Daniel Boone

Pioneer Trailblazer

by Jim Hargrove

CHILDRENS PRESS ®

CHICAGO

PICTURE ACKNOWLEDGMENTS

Historical Pictures Service, Chicago—Frontispiece, pages 60, 73, 74 (2 photos), 76, 78
Missouri Historical Society—pages 8, 77, 80 (bottom)
The Filson Club—Louisville, Kentucky—pages 34, 75
Roloc Color Slides—page 79 (2 photos)
State Historical Society of Wisconsin—page 80 (top)
Cover illustration by Len W. Meents

Library of Congress Cataloging in Publication Data

Hargrove, Jim.
    Daniel Boone: pioneer trailblazer.

    Includes index.
    Summary: Traces the life of the colonial pioneer, hunter, and woodsman, from his youth in the Pennsylvania wilderness to his adventures in the sparsely settled portions of Virginia, the Carolinas, Kentucky, and Missouri.
    1. Boone, Daniel, 1734-1820—Juvenile literature.
    2. Pioneers—Kentucky—Biography—Juvenile literature.
    3. Kentucky—Biography—Juvenile literature.
    4. Frontier and pioneer life—Kentucky—Juvenile literature.
    5. Kentucky—History—To 1792—Juvenile literature.
    [1. Boone, Daniel, 1734-1820. 2. Pioneers.
    3. Frontier and pioneer life] I. Title.
    F454.B66H37   1985   976.9′02′0924 [B] [92]   85-13309
    ISBN 0-516-03215-1

1 2 3 4 5 6 7 8 9 10 R 94 93 92 91 90 89 88 87 86 85

Table of Contents

Chapter 1
Almost Like an Indian Boy   9

Chapter 2
The Long Rifles   21

Chapter 3
A Frontier Family   35

Chapter 4
The Search for Kentucky   49

Chapter 5
The Wilderness Road   61

Chapter 6
The Long Handshake   81

Chapter 7
The Battle of Boonesborough   95

Chapter 8
Forever Westward   107

Time Line   116

Index   121

Chapter 1

ALMOST LIKE AN INDIAN BOY

Daniel opened the deerskin pouch hanging from the belt of his black-dyed trousers. He removed a small chunk of steel and a slightly smaller piece of flint rock. Quickly, he struck the flint against the steel a few inches above a pile of dry grass he had collected.

Each time he struck together the flint and steel, a few white-hot sparks fell onto the dried grass. After just a few tries, a small plume of smoke was rising from the tinder. He picked the grass up in his hands and blew gently on the glowing bits of straw. In a few more seconds, there was flame.

He dropped the flaming straw into a small fire pit he had prepared, and began placing small twigs, then larger ones, carefully over the fire. Soon he was cracking dead tree limbs into pieces and adding them to the fire. When it was blazing steadily in the hot summer sun, Daniel added an armful of green grass, smothering the flames. But the fire was not out. In a few seconds, billows of black smoke began to filter through the topmost layer of green grass.

The fire had been built just twenty yards or so upwind of the herd of cows Daniel was watching. In a few more

9

seconds, the first puffs of smoke drifted across the cattle. Daniel added another armful of grass to the fire. Then he walked to his rifle, which was leaning against a tree at the edge of the forest. His father had given him the rifle a year or two earlier, when Daniel was twelve years old. Already, he was an excellent shot and the most skilled hunter in the large Boone family.

Daniel tucked his short-barreled rifle under his arm and looked across the field where his cows were grazing. Several were slowly walking toward the smoky fire. Somehow, the cattle seemed to understand that the smoke would drive away flies and mosquitoes.

In the distance beyond the cows, Daniel could see the tiny log cabin where he and his mother, Sarah, spent each summer. Using a wooden churn near the cabin, Sarah would make butter out of the milk from the cows. When the fall came, Daniel and Sarah would drive the herd back to Exeter.

Daniel's real home, as well as those of his many relations, was in the tiny village of Exeter, about four miles away. Exeter was in eastern Pennsylvania, along the banks of the Schuylkill River. Today, the little village no longer exists, but the modern city of Reading, Pennsylvania, is nearby. When Daniel Boone was young—in the 1740s—the state of Pennsylvania did not yet exist.

Pennsylvania is a word that means "Penn's woods." *Penn*

comes from William Penn who founded a colony there and *silva* is the Latin word for woods. Daniel thought about the story his grandfather often told of how the Boone family came to Pennsylvania.

In the year 1681, Charles II, king of England, gave a huge tract of land in the New World to an Englishman named William Penn. Penn had not always been treated so nicely by the government of Charles II. Not long before he received the priceless gift, William Penn had been in an English jail. He was sent there because of the unusual views of his church, the Society of Friends, better known as the Quakers.

Many people in England were suspicious of the strange ways of the Quakers. Men and women in the Society of Friends believed in what they called "plain living." They wore simple clothes, usually dyed black. When they spoke, instead of saying the word "you," they said "thee" or "thou." Most important, they believed that the Church of England and its leaders were sinful. True Christians, the Quakers believed, would lead their own lives away from the Church of England.

When William Penn came to the New World in 1682 to see his land, a few English Quakers followed him. As the years passed, more English Quakers, as well as people from other European countries, began crossing the Atlantic Ocean to find a new life in Pennsylvania. In 1712, George Boone,

Daniel's grandfather, decided to send his three oldest children to America from their home in England. One of the children was Squire Boone, who would become Daniel's father.

The Boones were Quakers. William Penn had promised that all Quakers who moved to Pennsylvania would be treated well. He also made it possible for Quakers, and all settlers, to buy land very inexpensively. For about the same cost as a sailing ship ticket to cross the Atlantic Ocean, a settler in Pennsylvania could buy five thousand acres of land.

George Boone and the rest of his family followed the three children to the New World about five years later, arriving in Philadelphia in 1717.

By the following year, George Boone built a log home in Exeter. Many other Quakers also settled in the area. Daniel's grandfather became a leader in Exeter's Quaker church, and a justice of the peace. Daniel's father, Squire Boone, would also move to Exeter, but before he did he married a twenty-year-old girl named Sarah Morgan, who would become Daniel's mother. Squire and Sarah Boone had many children. Daniel was the sixth. He was born on November 2, 1734.

Daniel put another armload of fresh grass on the smoldering fire as he thought about his grandfather's interesting story. It saddened him to think how George Boone had died just a few months earlier. Suddenly, he heard a twig break in the forest. He grabbed the rifle and silently walked toward the woods.

"Thou hast better show thyself, Henry Miller," Daniel shouted at the invisible noisemaker, "or it will be a shot in the britches for thee." Daniel was almost certain that the sound was made by his friend from town. No Indian, intent on hiding, would walk so carelessly.

In a rush, Henry Miller appeared from between the trees and ran into the clearing. "Daniel Boone, thou must have ears like a deer," Henry said.

"And thou has feet like a buffalo," Daniel joked. The two friends put their arms on each other's shoulders and began to wrestle. Even though Henry was several years older, and a full head taller, Daniel soon tumbled him to the ground.

"There are fresh deer tracks crossing the Delaware trace," Henry said, getting to his feet. Delaware Indians, like the Shawnee, were familiar visitors in Exeter. An Indian trail, or trace, had been pounded into the forest floor just a few hundred yards from the clearing.

Daniel looked at the sun, still high in the sky, and at the cows, almost motionless in the clearing. "Besides," Henry continued, "some new buckskins would suit thee."

Although he wore the black clothing preferred by most Quakers, Daniel recently had taken to wrapping his legs with the tough skin of the male deer. Buckskin protected his legs and pants in the forest.

"Well, I guess we'd better bring it in," he answered. Daniel rarely missed a chance to hunt, and kill, the animals that lived around him. Today, this may seem cruel. But on the American frontier, when Daniel Boone was young and eastern Pennsylvania was the American west, it was a necessity.

The frontier forest supported many different kinds of animals. Bear, deer, rabbit, fox, even buffalo roamed the forests and meadows of eastern United States. Their skins could be made into warm coats for the winter, blankets for chilly nights, and rugs to place on the floors of frontier cabins. The meat could be roasted over an open fire, or cooked in soups and stews. Frontier families even found uses for animal bones. If the hunt were bad, it could mean death both for European settlers and native Indians in the American wilderness.

Throughout most of his long and fascinating life, Daniel Boone would be known, first and foremost, as a skilled hunter. As he grew older and moved west, many people would follow him. They knew that wherever he led them, he would find food to eat and the skins needed to stay alive during the cold winter months.

Other than Indians, no one was ever more at home in the wilderness than Daniel Boone. Much of what he knew about living on open land was learned from the Delaware and

Shawnee Indians of Pennsylvania. For the most part, the early Pennsylvania settlers lived peacefully with the Indians. Since childhood, Daniel had watched the Indians who visited his home in Exeter. He would listen to them speak with his father, Squire Boone, in a mixture of tongues, some words in an Indian language, others in English. When words would not do, his father and the visitors would tell stories with their hands and draw pictures in the dirt.

As he grew older, he realized how much he could learn from the Indian braves who hunted the woods of Pennsylvania. He learned many words in the Delaware and Shawnee languages. He sometimes even followed the braves on the hunt. He learned how to strip the bark off a tree, line it with leaves, twigs, and dirt, and crawl inside to stay warm in the forest.

From the Indians, he learned how to track an animal over the hardest ground, and how to cook meat so that the juices would keep it moist. Many of the people in Exeter thought it was peculiar that young Daniel seemed to want to live just like an Indian boy. But to Daniel it only seemed natural.

In later years, the settlers would fight gruesome wars with the Indians. When he had to, Daniel would join the battles. But unlike many of the European settlers around him, Daniel never became an Indian killer. He just had too many friends among the American natives.

When Daniel and Henry Miller reached the Indian trail,

Daniel saw that the deer tracks were several hours old. "Thou will be an old man with a beard before this deer is spotted," Daniel joked to his friend.

Henry knew that he was joking. They could probably find the deer, but it could take many hours. In the meantime, he would be missed back in Exeter, where he had a job working for Daniel's father, Squire Boone. Squire Boone had a blacksmith shop, where he built a furnace hot enough to melt and shape iron. He could shape horseshoes, mend iron animal traps, and even fix rifles, a skill that Daniel was learning as well. At Squire Boone's shop, Henry Miller was an apprentice.

"I had best be back at the shop," Henry said suddenly after the pair had made a few more steps along the Indian trace. "I'll come to see thee again next week." With that he was gone, and Daniel was alone in the thick forest.

His house may have been in the tiny village of Exeter, in Oley Township, but the wilderness was where he felt most at home. In town, most of the children would attend a makeshift school, but Daniel would not. Later in life, he would say that he never spent a single day in a schoolroom, and it was undoubtedly true. In a year or two, he would learn to read and write a bit from the wife of his older brother, Samuel. But he would never learn to spell properly.

Exeter might be the place for his family and friends, he thought, but not for him. Whenever he was at home, he talked about hunting, exploring, and woodcrafts. Near his father's house was the home of Mordecai Lincoln. Mordecai's grandson, Abraham, was about Daniel's age and a good friend as well. Daniel's friend Abe Lincoln was the grandfather of the famous Abraham Lincoln who became the sixteenth president of the United States. Like the Boones, the Lincoln family was large. Over the years, five different Lincolns would marry five different Boones.

At the time, of course, Daniel had no idea that his neighbors in Exeter would become such a famous family. Nor did he know that Henry Miller, partly because of what he learned at Squire Boone's blacksmith shop, would build the first iron mill in the colony of Virginia and become one of the richest men in America. Instead, Daniel was concentrating on something else.

Walking along the Indian trace, he had spotted something important. He didn't need to look too close at the markings in the soft ground to know what they were. They were bear tracks, and fresh!

As twilight came, Sarah Boone looked across the field where the cows were still grazing. Her son was nowhere in sight. She called his name, but there was no answer. It wasn't unusual for Daniel to be away from the cows. He often hunted in the woods beyond the clearing. In the darkness, Sarah herded the cattle closer to the tiny cabin. Inside the rough shelter, she ate a late dinner of rabbit stew and began to worry.

By the next morning, Daniel still had not returned. Shortly after dawn, Sarah walked and ran to Exeter to organize a search party. Several of the townsfolk hurriedly packed some food and water and headed into the hills in search of Daniel.

The search party couldn't find a trace of the young boy in the hills and forests of Oley Township. So they headed south toward Neversink Mountain, but it grew dark and the party was forced to make camp. The next morning they were off again.

During the afternoon of the second day, they saw smoke from a campfire on Neversink Mountain. After several more hours of difficult travel, the party finally reached the campfire. There they found young Daniel Boone, sitting comfortably under a bark shelter, eating bear meat. The rest of the bear, already skinned and cut up into pieces, was hanging from wooden poles nearby.

"Boy," one of the men from the town said sternly, "we thought thee must be lost."

"I'm not lost," Daniel answered. "I'm right here on the south shoulder of Neversink Mountain, nine miles from the cabin. Maybe nine and a half miles."

The men looked at each other and grumbled. "Sarah Boone is sick with worry, young man," another one said.

"I am sorry for the trouble I have caused." Daniel answered. "I was tracking a bear and, as thee can see, I have found it. Join me. There is plenty to eat for all." It was difficult for any of the tired men to argue with the fourteen-year-old boy's logic.

For the next two years the Boones remained in Oley Township. Squire Boone continued working as a blacksmith and grew vegetables in the rich farmland of the Schuylkill valley. Daniel and his many brothers and sisters (Squire and Sarah Boone had eleven children in all) did their share to help out in the blacksmith shop, the farm, and the house.

Squire Boone began to have problems with the Quaker church. Two different times, members of his family married people who did not belong to the Society of Friends. This was considered a sin by the Quakers. Squire refused to criticize his children for the marriages, as he was required to do by the Quaker rules, and he was eventually expelled from the church.

There was another problem as well. More and more people were coming to the Schuylkill valley to build homes and buy farmland. Squire Boone realized that it would be difficult for his children to find good farmland nearby.

In 1750, after many long talks with his family, Squire Boone sold all his land in Pennsylvania. He placed a few of his household goods and blacksmith tools in a covered wagon and prepared to move on. Joining the traveling family were two of Daniel's cousins and Squire Boone's apprentice, Henry Miller.

Chapter 2

THE LONG RIFLES

The Boone family left Pennsylvania without knowing where they would settle. To the west were the rugged Allegheny Mountains, impossible to cross with a covered wagon. To the south were the Blue Ridge Mountains, and a bit to the west were more of the high Alleghenies.

As they traveled south and west, the Boones followed the banks of a number of rivers, natural passageways through the hills and mountains. Where the Shenandoah and Potomac rivers met, about fifty miles northwest of Washington, D.C., a man named Robert Harper carried the family across the Potomac and into Virginia aboard his ferryboat. More than a century later, the town of Harper's Ferry would be an important battleground in the Civil War.

The Shenandoah valley was becoming an important route between the mountains for American settlers, but it hadn't been so for long. The first colonists, a group of Virginians led by Alexander Spotswood, arrived there just thirty-five years earlier, on September 5, 1716. Before, the valley had been traveled only by Indians. *Shenandoah* is an Indian word meaning "daughter of the stars."

Daniel Boone was sixteen years old when his family

settled in for a brief stay in the Shenandoah valley of Virginia. Squire Boone did some farming and blacksmithing. But Daniel and his friend Henry Miller wanted none of the quiet farmer's life. Soon, they were off on the hunting trail.

Sometime earlier Daniel had traded his short, European-style rifle for a long rifle made in Pennsylvania. The barrel of the early frontier's most famous weapon was more than three feet long. The long barrel allowed hunters to shoot more accurately than before possible.

This type of rifle, also called a flintlock, did not shoot bullets as we know them today. In order to make a single shot, it was necessary to first clean out the barrel with a piece of cloth and a long stick called a ramrod. Then, a small amount of gunpowder had to be carefully measured out and poured into the barrel. Next, a small metal ball—the bullet— was placed in a small square of cloth that was usually moistened with saliva. The bullet and cloth were then rammed all the way into the barrel so that the cloth pushed against the gunpowder.

After all this, the rifle was still not ready to fire. A bit more gunpowder had to be placed in a small part of the barrel called the flash pan. Then, the hammer was pulled back on the rifle and locked into place. Attached to the hammer was a small piece of flint. When the trigger was pulled, the hammer would be released. The flint would strike against a piece of steel, called the striker plate, and make a small shower of sparks. If all went right, a spark or two would fall through a small hole in the barrel and detonate the charge of gunpowder behind the cloth and steel ball, propelling the projectile out of the barrel.

This type of gun was used from the late 1600s until well into the 1800s. It is the weapon that was used by both the Americans and British during the revolutionary war. And it was the gun that the earliest pioneers, like Daniel Boone, carried west.

Daniel and Henry Miller carried their long rifles far from Squire Boone's temporary home in the Shenandoah valley of Virginia. They traveled 150 miles southwest, to another valley formed by the Yadkin River of North Carolina. The two young hunters were delighted by the amount of game they found along the river. Deer, elk, buffalo, bear, and many kinds of smaller animals were plentiful.

For the better part of a year, Daniel and Henry hunted in the Yadkin valley. Daniel no longer wore the black clothes of the Quakers. In the wilderness, where he would spend much of his life, he had taken to wearing pants and shirts made of buckskin. His moccasins were made of deerskin. The soft shoes allowed him to walk silently in the woods.

From deerskin he also made pouches to carry his lead shot and food. On the trail food was usually deer jerky, deer meat dried over a smoky fire to keep it from spoiling. He carried the most precious of all his supplies, gunpowder, in a hollow animal horn. Even in rain, the powder horn would keep its contents dry. "Keep your powder dry" was a well-known expression on the American frontier. Wet gunpowder was worthless.

Daniel and Henry loaded the animal skins they had collected onto packhorses and made the long trip back to Pennsylvania. There, they sold their catch for more than a thousand dollars. After vacationing in luxury for several weeks, they headed back toward the Shenandoah valley of Virginia, where Daniel's family was still living. They brought along fresh supplies of gunpowder, hunting knives, and gifts for everyone. And they told fantastic stories of their adventures in the Yadkin valley.

"Never have we seen such game," Daniel told his father when he reached the little cabin along the Shenandoah. "We didn't even have to track the critters. We just sat for a spell and waited quietly. Soon enough, they'd be along for sure."

Daniel also told Squire Boone about the wide-open land in North Carolina, where there was plenty of elbow room for farmers and hunters alike. By the fall of 1751, the father was convinced by his son. Although Henry Miller remained behind to make his fortune in Virginia, the Boones decided to move on once again.

As they had before, Daniel and his family moved south and west, following a trail between the mountains. When they finally arrived on the Yadkin, winter was hard upon them. With little money to buy land, and no time to build a house, they were forced to spend the entire winter living in a cave above the river.

The next spring, Squire Boone and his children built a rough cabin on land they did not own. But no sooner was the shelter completed than Daniel was back again on the hunting trail.

One of the settlers along the Yadkin River remarked that Daniel could shoot a tick—a tiny insect—off a bear's nose a hundred yards away. Daniel enjoyed the story and started calling his long rifle "Ticklicker." During the summer and fall of 1752, Daniel and Ticklicker hunted and trapped many animals. He was able to sell the skins, and some of the meat, at the little town of Salisbury for a fair amount of money.

By the following year, Daniel had earned enough money to help his father buy 640 acres of land along the Yadkin River, and soon an equal amount of property on the opposite side of the river. He purchased the land from an Englishman, the Earl of Granville, who, like a number of his countrymen before him, had been granted huge amounts of land in the Carolinas by the king of England.

In North Carolina, as well as in a number of other colonies and communities on the western frontier, there were four major groups of people who would be involved in a struggle that would last about three decades. The struggle would end in the birth of the United States of America. Daniel Boone would play an important role throughout the long fight.

The people who would fight over the land that would become the United States were native American Indians; Frenchmen, who claimed a large expanse of land including the Ohio and Mississippi river valleys; the English and European colonists (excluding Spaniards and Frenchmen), who had settled in the original thirteen colonies; and American colonists, American-born descendants of European settlers. In the end, all but the American colonists would lose.

The Indians, of course, were the first people to live on the land. The colonists who crossed the Atlantic from England and other European countries lived on land claimed by the king of England. It was no surprise when the Indians sometimes disagreed with the English king's right to claim the land for his subjects.

Soldiers in the English army, often called Redcoats because of their bright uniforms, offered some protection to settlers along the Atlantic coast. But the English army did not follow the earliest pioneers, like Daniel Boone, west. The handful of British soldiers in tiny forts along the frontier could not protect colonists from Indian raids. Nevertheless, the English expected all European settlers on the American frontier to pay taxes to England.

When he bought his land on the Yadkin River, Squire

Boone was expected to pay taxes to the English every year, to give them most of the gold and silver he might find on his land, and to clear and farm twenty additional acres of land every three years. If he did not do so, his land would be taken away.

Relations between the settlers and the Indians were not as good in North Carolina as they had been in Pennsylvania. Although the Catawba Indians were generally friendly when the Boones came to their area, the Shawnee were not. Squire Boone and the other settlers along the Yadkin knew that the taxes they paid to England would do little to protect them from Indian raids.

There was another danger as well. Most of the land east of the Allegheny Mountains in America was claimed by England. But west of the mountains French traders and trappers roamed freely. The vast territory claimed by the French went from the Alleghenies in the east to the Rocky Mountains in the west. Anyone traveling across the mountains west of the Yadkin River could be attacked not only by Indians, but by French soldiers as well.

The French had little interest in settling and farming the land they claimed was theirs. Instead, they wanted to hunt the animals that were found there, collecting the valuable furs. But they saw the handful of American colonists who were already crossing the mountains as a threat to the game they hunted.

A year or two before the Boones moved to the Yadkin valley, the French and English began a serious quarrel over who controlled the enormous Ohio River valley. In 1753, a young officer in the colonial army named George Washington visited a French fort near the Ohio River to demand that the French soldiers leave British land.

When the French soldiers refused to leave, a number of American colonists, many from Virginia, organized a trip to build their own fort on the Ohio River. They decided to build their fort at a place called the Forks of the Ohio where the Allegheny and Monongahela rivers joined to form the Ohio River. The site was nearly three hundred miles north of Daniel's home on the Yadkin River, but he would soon feel its influence.

As soon as the tiny fort was completed, the colonists were attacked by French troops. The French and Indian War had begun.

The French soldiers conquered the Americans and built a huge new fort, which they called Fort Duquesne, at the Forks of the Ohio. Too late, an army of soldiers from Virginia, under George Washington's command, discovered what had happened. About fifty miles from the captured fort, Washington fought his first battle with French soldiers. The Virginians built a small fort, which Washington called Fort Necessity, but were soon forced to surrender to the French.

During the summer of 1754, battles between the French and English forces began all up and down the American frontier. Even on the Yadkin River, three hundred miles south of the Ohio valley, the struggle between the two European nations could be felt. At about the same time Washington and his troops were struggling in Pennsylvania, a group of Shawnee Indians attacked a tiny town near the Boone homestead on the Yadkin. When the friendly Catawba Indians helped the settlers drive the attackers away, it was discovered that the Shawnee were carrying French rifles.

Now the settlers knew that the French were using Indians to attack frontier towns. French soldiers and traders told the Indians west of the mountains that white settlers under English rule would soon be invading their lands and killing their game. Many Indian groups feared the American homesteaders more than the French hunters. They agreed to work with the French to rid their land of English control.

When it was clear that war was at hand, Daniel Boone joined the North Carolina army and prepared to fight the French. He was twenty years old. Daniel's job in the Army was to drive a supply wagon and to work as a blacksmith. Of course, when the army reached Fort Duquesne at the Forks of the Ohio, Daniel would have to fight like any other soldier.

Early in 1755, a British general named Edward Braddock arrived to take command of the colonial forces. Starting in Maryland and heading toward the Forks of the Ohio,

Braddock's army would have to cross the Allegheny Mountains.

In June, 1755, the army began the terrible trip. In the lead were British Redcoats, professional soldiers from England under Braddock's direct command. Next in the endless line of troops were the colonial forces, soldiers from America led by George Washington. Behind the marching soldiers followed more than a hundred horse-drawn wagons, carrying food, weapons, medicine, and other necessities. Driving one of the wagons was Daniel Boone.

Braddock made a poor decision when he decided to try to bring wagons over the steep Allegheny Mountains. It took more than a month for the army to cross the thickly forested terrain, and the wagons always slowed the progress. This would not be the last poor decision Braddock would make.

Throughout the month of June, the army struggled through the forests and mountains of Pennsylvania. During the day, the soldiers faced backbreaking work, cutting paths through the forest for the wagons to follow. At sunset, the exhausted soldiers gathered around campfires to eat, rest, and tell stories.

During these times, Daniel made friends with a wagon driver who was traveling with the forces from Pennsylvania. This man's last name has been spelled many different ways by historians: Finley, Findley, and Findlay are some. In the first book ever written about Daniel Boone, *The Dis-*

covery, Settlement and Present State of Kentucke published in 1784 and read by Boone himself, this friend is called John Finley, the author.

John Finley played an important role in Daniel Boone's life. During the long march toward the Forks of the Ohio and Fort Duquesne, young soldiers crowded around Finley to hear his magical tales of a faraway land, hidden by mountains, called Kentucky. No one listened to the stories more closely than Daniel Boone.

Finley, who roamed the frontier trading goods with Indians and settlers alike, was one of perhaps a half-dozen non-Indians who had ever set foot in Kentucky. He had collected a fortune in furs there, only to have them stolen by Indians when he was carrying them back east. The soil was so rich and the rainfall so generous in Kentucky, he said, that Indian corn practically jumped out of the ground, and meadowlands of bluegrass flourished.

Daniel never forgot the stories John Finley told about Kentucky. But by the early days of July in 1755, the time for storytelling was over. The army of General Braddock was finally nearing Fort Duquesne. During the difficult march across the Allegheny Mountains, many of the soldiers had become sick. One of the men who was ill with fever was George Washington who, as a young commander at the time, was just two years older than Daniel Boone.

Braddock led his troops across the Monongahela River on

July 9, readying his men for the final attack on Fort Duquesne. But before he reached the fort, nearly a thousand French soldiers and Indian braves attacked him from the woods.

Daniel Boone drove his wagon across the Monongahela hours after the first troops had crossed it. From his position at the rear of the army he could not see what was happening, although he probably heard the gunfire ahead. Soon enough, it became all too clear that the battle was not going well.

British soldiers never seemed to understand how to fight in the American wilderness. At the first sign of an ambush, Braddock had ordered his soldiers to stand in straight lines out in the open and fire on command at an enemy completely hidden by the trees. His army was soon cut to pieces by French and Indian fire. Two decades later, British soldiers would begin losing the American Revolution in much the same way.

Even though he was seriously ill, Washington knew better than to stand in the open and wait to be shot. He ordered his colonial troops into the woods where the thick trees would give some protection against the hail of French and Indian gunfire.

But the move was too late. General Braddock was shot and would soon die. More than half of the British Redcoats were soon dead or wounded as well. Even Washington's better-protected forces could not stop the French soldiers and the screaming Indians who charged forward, directly toward Daniel Boone.

On every side, Daniel saw the panicked soldiers running away from the advancing French and Indians.

"Stay with your wagons!" yelled one of the commanders. Daniel couldn't help but notice that the commander seemed to be heading for the hills. But Daniel stayed. And the French and Indians came closer.

Finally, he could wait no longer. He took out his knife and cut the straps fastening the horses to his wagon. He leaped onto the back of one of the horses and galloped away, along with the other wagon drivers who were still alive. One of them was John Finley. Some years later, the two friends would meet again.

In the meantime, Daniel had had his fill of war.

Mrs. Daniel Boone

Chapter 3

A FRONTIER FAMILY

Since Daniel Boone's time, hundreds of stories have been told about him. Many of them are exaggerated, and this is hardly surprising. On the American frontier, few people wrote about the things they saw and heard. Instead, the pioneers shared their adventures through oral tradition, passing on stories to their children and grandchildren.

Thus arose the story of how Daniel met Rebecca Bryan, the girl who became his wife. When walking in the forest one spring day, the story went, Daniel saw an enormous pair of eyes shining from between the trees. Only a deer could have such deep, dark eyes, he supposedly thought.

Daniel hurriedly poured powder into his long rifle, the story continued, and pressed the round shot into the barrel. He primed the flash pan, raised his rifle, and fired.

The black eyes blinked as the gunpowder flashed, but the shot flew harmlessly above its mark. An instant later, a slender, black-haired girl rushed into the clearing. She was the daughter of Joseph Bryan, a settler who had come to the Yadkin River from Pennsylvania sometime before the Boones arrived.

This story of how Daniel Boone and Rebecca Bryan met is

probably exaggerated. But it is known that he met Rebecca before he left to fight in his first battle of the French and Indian War. The Bryans were the wealthiest family in the Yadkin valley. The year before his first taste of war, Daniel's sister Mary married William Bryan, a member of Rebecca's large family.

After the defeat of the British and American army in Pennsylvania, Daniel hurried back to his father's cabin on the Yadkin. There, he wasted little time in proposing to Rebecca.

The Bryan and Boone families were already firm friends. Although the Boones were not as wealthy as the Bryans, Squire Boone was highly regarded throughout the Yadkin valley. He served as justice of the peace, and was well known by most of the early settlers. And Daniel, even in his early twenties, was considered to be a superb hunter and marksman and an honest, witty man. The romance between Daniel and Rebecca must have pleased both families.

As a justice of the peace, Squire Boone married Daniel and Rebecca on August 14, 1756. Rebecca was sixteen or seventeen years old; Daniel was twenty-one. The newlyweds moved into a tiny cabin Daniel had built on his father's land near the Yadkin. There, the couple's first two sons, James and Israel, were born. In all, they would have nine children, but there would be many moves and much high adventure before the last child was born in 1781.

For several years, Daniel settled down with his growing family to hunt and farm the land around his little cabin. It was a quiet and peaceful time that would not last. By the spring of 1758, less than two years after his marriage, the French and Indian War once again took Daniel away from his home.

Like most settlers, Daniel was not entirely happy with the British rule of the American colonies. For one thing, the British made people on the frontier pay taxes and offered little in return. Many frontiersmen were also increasingly unhappy with the court systems set up by British rulers. They felt many of the courts and judges treated people unfairly. Soon, a new kind of frontier justice would arise in North Carolina and elsewhere to combat corrupt judges and politicians.

Despite their problems with the British, however, settlers in the western portions of the colonies saw the French as an even greater problem. French hunters and traders were determined to keep Americans out of their hunting grounds. Worse yet, for years the French had tried, with some success, to turn the Indians against the settlers. Many Indian raids were inspired by the French.

By 1758, the British were more determined than ever to drive the French out of North America. Early that year, a British general named John Forbes began to organize an army for a second attack on Fort Duquesne, the French fortress at the Forks of the Ohio. Once again, George Washington was in charge of the colonial troops.

As soon as news of the coming attack reached the Yadkin valley, Daniel joined the North Carolina troops. Rebecca and the two young boys would live with the Bryans while Daniel was gone. As he had in the earlier assault against the French fort, Daniel served as driver of a supply wagon.

The first attempt to drive the French from the Ohio valley had ended in disaster for the British and American troops. British commanders and politicians were determined to win in their second attack. The army organized by Forbes and Washington was even larger than the first. More important, the British and Americans had learned a valuable lesson from the French.

While the army of which Daniel Boone was a part was marching through Pennsylvania, the British held meetings with many different tribes of Indians. At each meeting the British gave the Indians shiny beads, sometimes woven into belts, that the Indians often used as a kind of money called *wampum*. The British also promised that if the French were driven out of the Ohio valley, the settlers would not be allowed to move there. Once again, stated the British, the land west of the Alleghenies would belong only to the Indians.

Many Indians appreciated the gifts and promises of the British. Some agreed to fight against the French. And many who were fighting for the French decided to leave their former friends. These changes doomed the presence of the French in America.

The vast army, with John Forbes and George Washington at the front and Daniel Boone and his wagon at the rear, reached the Forks of the Ohio near the end of November, 1758. On the evening before the planned attack, the French realized that they were hopelessly outnumbered. They burned Fort Duquesne to the ground and detonated whatever ammunition they could not carry away.

Without a shot being fired, British and American colonists took charge of the Ohio valley. The soldiers would build a new fort at the Forks of the Ohio. In honor of the prime minister of England, William Pitt, the new fort would be named Fort Pitt. Over the years, the city of Pittsburgh would grow up around it.

The French would fight more battles in America, but by the early 1760s French forces would be driven away completely. As for the promises made by the British to the Indians, few would be kept. British rulers would be unable, and at times unwilling, to keep settlers from moving across the Allegheny Mountains and settling on the rich plains to the west. One group of those settlers would be the family of Daniel Boone.

Daniel returned to the Yadkin River hoping that his days at war were over. They were not. Although sent away from

Fort Duquesne, small numbers of French soldiers and hunters were still trying to turn the Indians against the settlers. Their arguments caused great unrest among the Cherokee Indians, who began making a series of raids against settlers in the Yadkin valley.

Throughout 1759 and 1760, wars with the Cherokee Indians raged on the North Carolina frontier. Many settlers, as well as Indians, were killed. Several times, Daniel and Rebecca took their small children to a fort some miles west of their cabin while the Cherokee were on the warpath.

When the fort itself was attacked by Cherokee early in 1760, Rebecca felt that they had stayed in unfriendly territory long enough. As soon as spring weather arrived, the young family began a trip of more than two hundred miles northeast to the relative safety of Culpepper, Virginia.

For a time, Daniel tried to settle down in Culpepper. He worked as a wagon driver, carrying tobacco to Fredericksburg, which was near George Washington's Mount Vernon home. Although they had served together in the French and Indian War, Boone and Washington had never met. But in Fredericksburg they did meet, Daniel introducing himself as a young soldier who had been in Washington's colonial army.

Rebecca and her growing family stayed in Virginia for about two years, but Daniel could not stay put. After a long hunting trip, he learned that a large army of soldiers was being organized to try to end the war with the Cherokee Indians. Once again he joined the fight. By November of 1760, the war was over. The Cherokee had lost, and the chiefs signed a peace treaty that would make it safe for settlers to return to the frontier.

Although the fighting was over, Daniel did not return directly to his family in Virginia. He spent the winter hunting and trapping. During the spring of 1761, he returned to his cabin on the Yadkin River and planted a crop. He harvested it that fall and finally began the long trip back to Virginia.

During the Cherokee wars, many of the settlers in the Yadkin valley had fled to Virginia to escape the bitter fighting. Among the refugees were Sarah and Squire Boone, Daniel's mother and father. When Daniel arrived in Virginia with news that he had meat and grain stockpiled in the Yadkin valley, all the Boones were anxious to return to their homes in North Carolina.

They did not wait until spring to make their move. Before the first months of 1762, Daniel and Rebecca, Squire and Sarah, and all of the Boones' many relations were back in their cabins along the Yadkin. But by spring the Boones would find that the years of brutal Indian wars on the frontier had changed the once peaceful valley.

Not only farmers and hunters returned to the Yadkin following the defeat of the Cherokee. People who had no interest in the values of decency and hard work—values once commonly accepted by almost everyone along the Yadkin—now were coming to the valley. For the first time, settlers were troubled by horse thieves, cattle rustlers, and bandits. Gangs of outlaws, hiding in the mountains around the Yadkin valley by day, would sneak into the settlements at night to steal anything of value.

Once again, the British government was unable to stop the activities of outlaws along the frontier. Even when lawbreakers were caught, they could often bribe judges into letting them go. Angered by a powerless government and corrupt courts, some of the people along the Yadkin decided to take matters into their own hands.

These people called themselves Regulators. Many times during the 1760s and early 1770s, bands of Regulators from North Carolina took it upon themselves to enforce the law and punish judges and lawyers they felt were unfair. When they caught people they thought were horse thieves or robbers, some groups of Regulators often hanged them without a trial. Several times, they even attacked judges and lawyers from the courthouse at Salisbury, beating them up and burning their crops in the fields.

Daniel Boone understood the many injustices brought about by the British-ruled courts on the frontier, but he wanted no part of the Regulation movement. For one thing, he understood that punishing people without a fair trial could lead to serious mistakes. Also, several of his friends became victims of the Regulators.

One of his friends was a judge named Richard Henderson who frequently held court in Salisbury. Daniel had met the judge through his father, who also often worked at the courthouse as a justice of the peace. Squire Boone and Richard Henderson were friends, and Daniel and the judge also took a liking to one another.

During a court case one summer, Richard Henderson made a decision that angered the North Carolina Regulators. An angry mob appeared at the courthouse and drove the judge from his bench. That night, Regulators wearing masks to hide their faces burned down the judge's house and set fire to his crops in the field.

The mob action made Daniel angry. Richard Henderson had been a very good friend to him. Before many a long hunt, Daniel borrowed money from people to buy ammunition, supplies, and packhorses. When the hunt went well, he was able to repay the money he had borrowed. But more than once many of his skins, supplies, and horses were stolen by Indians. During these times, it was simply impossible for him to repay his debts.

Although Rebecca and the children did some farming on their land along the Yadkin, the food they grew was hardly enough to pay off debts. But Richard Henderson defended Daniel in court, often giving him more time to pay his debts.

And the two men enjoyed talking about the wilderness to the west of the Yadkin River.

Daniel told Richard Henderson the stories he had heard about the land the Indians called "Kentucke." He told the judge how he had met John Finley and the magical stories Finley had told about Kentucky. Henderson thought about trying to buy the land from the Indians.

Daniel and the judge made an agreement. Whenever Daniel made a long hunting trip across the mountains west of the Yadkin, he would keep notes about the land. He also would listen to stories from other hunters about the fabled land of Kentucky. Eventually, it was hoped, the two men would become partners, buying land in Kentucky and selling it to settlers.

By 1764 Daniel's eldest son James was seven, old enough to go hunting with his father. Daniel began taking James on many trips into the wilderness, teaching him many of his outdoorsman's secrets. He showed James how to always stay downwind of game, so the animals couldn't smell him coming. He showed him where natural salt deposits—often called "licks"—could be found, frequently near riverbanks. When animals came to lick the salt, they became easy targets for the long rifle.

Whenever he was at home in the Yadkin valley, Daniel would visit his friend Richard Henderson. The talk would soon turn to Kentucky.

"I reckon it's time to find Kentucke and put 'er on the map," Daniel told his friend. But Henderson was not ready to pay for an expedition to find the fabled land.

"You know what the Crown has said, Daniel," the judge answered, speaking of the English king. In 1763, George III, king of England, had ordered that all lands west of the mountains in the New World should belong to the Indians. The order was part of the settlement of the French and Indian War.

"But even George Washington says, privately of course, that American settlers have to keep coming westward," Daniel answered. "Besides, we're not just taking the land. We'll pay the Indians fair and square for it." Despite Daniel's arguments, Henderson was not yet ready to make a move.

Daniel loved the wilderness, and his love of the wild land was probably the force behind his desire to explore Kentucky. In the meantime, more and more settlers were coming into the Yadkin valley. Daniel decided to move his family farther upstream to escape what he considered to be congestion. In 1764 and 1765 he moved several times, each time building a cabin deeper in the mountains northwest of his earlier home.

Daniel and James hunted the mountains around their new homes. Daniel was happy to be away from the "crowded" lower Yadkin River, but whenever he had idle time, his thoughts turned to Kentucky. Early in the summer of 1765, Daniel and James made a two-month hunting trip in the mountains west of the upper Yadkin. When it was over, Daniel declared that James was as good an outdoorsman as his father.

Shortly after father and son returned to their cabin, Daniel learned about a new adventure. Five soldiers who had fought in the French and Indian War with Daniel stopped by. They were on their way to explore Florida, they said, and wondered if Daniel would like to come along.

Until just two years earlier, the land that is now the state of Florida was claimed by Spain. On February 10, 1763, England, France, and Spain signed the first Treaty of Paris, which ended the Seven Years' War in Europe and the French and Indian War in America. As part of that treaty, Spain gave Florida to England. Soon, the new British governor of Florida was inviting American settlers to come south to the new English territory.

Daniel quickly agreed to make the trip along with his friends from the war and several of his relatives. They began their journey in the fall, following the borders of South Carolina and Georgia southward. Over much of the trip they followed the Traders' Trace, a trail that had once been an Indian warpath.

But as the explorers traveled farther south, Daniel noticed that game became harder to find. The land grew swampy, swarming with mosquitoes and other stinging insects. By the time the party neared Florida, the food was gone entirely. Deer, bear, rabbits, and other game so plentiful in the north seemed completely absent in the land near Florida.

Daniel and his friends were sick with fever and nearly starving when they stumbled upon a Seminole Indian village. The kind Indians saw that their visitors were in trouble. They gave Daniel and his friends food, and put medicine on their insect bites. In a few days, the men were strong enough to continue their journey, and the Seminoles gave them more dried food for the trip.

Daniel and the rest of his party explored Florida from St. Augustine west to Pensacola, on the Gulf of Mexico. By the time they reached the old Spanish town of Pensacola, it was already late fall. Daniel had never been in the tropical south. He was delighted by the warm waters of the Gulf of Mexico. And he felt that a land rarely touched by cold weather even during the winter must be paradise.

Daniel bought a small house and some land in Pensacola. He gave up the last of his money for a down payment, and signed a letter promising to pay the rest later. But as he headed home for the Yadkin valley, he noticed once more that the land was without game. What would he hunt? What would his family eat? Suddenly, he began to realize that Florida was not the paradise he sought.

Daniel arrived at his cabin along the upper Yadkin late on

Christmas Day, 1765, just in time for Christmas dinner as he had promised Rebecca he would. He told her and his children about his adventures in the south. And then he told his growing family about the insects and lack of game in Florida. All agreed that the new land was not for them.

Chapter 4

THE SEARCH FOR KENTUCKY

In the summer of 1766, four hunters from the Yadkin valley crossed the Appalachian Mountains and traveled all the way to the Mississippi River. Two were Daniel's relative Benjamin Cutbirth and Daniel's brother-in-law John Stuart, and the other two were young hunters named John Baker and James Ward. The men had asked Daniel to come with them, but he had decided to stay closer to Rebecca and his family.

The four hunters became the first American settlers to travel overland to the Mississippi. Daniel spent the following year near the Yadkin, all the time wishing he had joined the exciting expedition west. By the fall of 1767, he could stand it no longer. After harvesting their small crops, Daniel and two of his friends from the Florida trip decided to cross the mountains and find the famous land called Kentucky.

It was not a good time to begin such a trip across the mountains. Winter was fast approaching. When the first big snows came, Daniel and his friends were forced to build an emergency cabin to wait out the worst of the winter months.

When spring came, the men pushed on, following river

valleys that snaked through the steep mountains. Where were the lush green meadows of Kentucky that John Finley had described years earlier? Game was everywhere, and the explorers had no difficulty hunting food and skins. But these thickly forested mountains were hardly paradise.

Finally, with no end to the mountains in sight, Daniel and his companions decided to turn back. They did not realize that they were already in eastern Kentucky. Had they traveled west for a few more days, the mountains would have ended and the meadows of bluegrass would have opened up before them.

Daniel returned to his family somewhat discouraged, but his great supply of meat and skins collected in the hills of eastern Kentucky at least made the trip partly worthwhile. Daniel settled down again, making short hunting trips with his son and farming the land in the Yadkin valley.

The following year, 1768, an old friend came to visit. He was John Finley, the man who had driven a wagon with Daniel in the French and Indian War and who had first told exciting stories about Kentucky. Finley arrived at Daniel's cabin driving a wagon loaded with cloth, needles, pots and pans, and other wares he traded with Indians and settlers.

The two old friends talked about their experiences in the war and about their more recent adventures. Soon enough, the talk turned to Kentucky. Over the years, Daniel had gradually given up the Quaker speech patterns of his youth, no longer using the pronouns "thee" or "thou."

"I reckon it's beyond me how you found those meadows," Daniel told his friend. "All we saw were mountains and more mountains. You'd have to be a mountain critter or a bird to get to Kentucke."

John Finley smiled and moved a little closer to the fire blazing in the fireplace of Daniel's cabin. Rebecca and the children listened along with Daniel. "There is a way, though," Finley answered at last. "The Indians call it 'Ouasioto.' It's a gap, a gap in the mountains. There's practically a highway through it. Indian warriors have used it for years. And I can find it."

"And can you find a way to keep our scalps on?" Daniel asked with a grin. "They ain't always too glad to see us palefaces coming across the mountains."

Daniel knew that there was no good answer to his question. But he also knew that few settlers were as skilled as he was in dealing with the Indians. He knew a few words in many different Indian languages. Some Indians had nicknamed him "Wide-Mouth."

Since winter was approaching, Daniel invited John Finley to stay with him and his family through the coldest months. Finley happily accepted. During the evenings around the fire, the two men made their plans to explore Kentucky in the spring.

In March of 1769, Daniel had to go to court to defend

himself against another suit for a debt he could not pay. The judge was his old friend Richard Henderson, who still was interested in Kentucky himself. Judge Henderson gave Daniel more time to pay the money he owed. Then he gave Daniel some of his own money to pay for the expedition to Kentucky.

On May 1, 1769, Daniel, John Finley, and four other men left Daniel's cabin on the upper Yadkin. Daniel's brother, Squire, followed a few months later. They were bound for Kentucky. Rebecca and her family were not worried about Daniel leaving. New vegetables were already growing in the garden. James, almost a teenager, was an expert hunter and could supply the family with plenty of raccoon, wild turkey, and even bear and deer.

The men traveled west, crossing high mountains through Moccasin Gap, crossing the Clinch River, and climbing over mountains with names like Walden's Ridge and Powell Mountain. When they were within twenty-five miles of the great gap they were seeking, they were shocked to find a settlement of colonists in the wilderness.

The people in the wilderness town were from Virginia. Led by a man named Joseph Martin, the pioneers welcomed Daniel and his group and told them that the great gap was just ahead. To their knowledge, no settlers had moved any farther west.

The great gap in the mountains leading into Kentucky

from the east is called Cumberland Gap today. After Daniel and his friends passed through it, they followed the old Indian trail, well worn by warriors over the years, for many miles. When the explorers arrived at the Cumberland River, they finally left the Indian trail and headed north. As they traveled, the mountains grew smaller.

Finally, the mountains disappeared entirely. Before the hearty band stretched grass-covered plains. At last they had found the fabled meadows of Kentucky. All kinds of game, and enormous herds—or droves—of buffalo were everywhere.

Describing the huge numbers of buffalo they saw, Daniel later said: "Sometimes we saw hundreds in a drove, and the numbers about the salt springs were amazing." In the promised land at last, the men decided to split up and explore different areas of Kentucky.

John Finley and three of the men continued west. Daniel and John Stuart headed north to explore the land around the Kentucky River. Behind them they left a simple camp, where they agreed to meet sometime later. But before the explorers could meet again at the camp, all would have difficulties with the Indians of Kentucky.

The party led by Finley met a band of Indians who took all the skins and furs they had collected on the trip. Daniel and John Stuart, while still near the Kentucky River, were captured by an Indian hunting party and held captive for a week. They finally managed to escape, but when they got back to the camp where all were supposed to meet, they found that it had been discovered by other Indians.

Nothing was left of their supplies. Finley and his party had gone home. Fortunately, there was plenty of game to hunt, and Daniel and John Stuart were able to provide themselves with fresh meat. Several times, Daniel's brother Squire made trips to the camp, bringing food and provisions.

Once, when Squire was back in North Carolina gathering more supplies, John Stuart was hunting alone. He was surprised by a hunting party of Indians, probably Cherokee, and was killed. Daniel was left alone in the wilderness without a dog, horse, even bread, salt, or sugar.

Although he had few supplies, Daniel continued exploring the land of Kentucky. He traveled as far north as the Ohio River, today the northern boundary of the state of Kentucky. He followed the valleys of other rivers as well, including the Kentucky and Licking rivers. Before long, Daniel knew more about the new land than any other explorer.

Daniel had been away from Rebecca and his family for nearly two years. Much of that time Daniel explored alone. He decided finally to break camp and head back home in March of 1771. Daniel and Squire loaded the valuable furs they had collected in Kentucky onto packhorses. After passing over the Cumberland Gap they made camp, then continued their journey eastward the next morning.

At their camp the following evening, they were surprised by a half dozen Cherokee warriors. The Indians did not harm the travelers, but took their rifles, their supplies, and, worse yet, all the furs they were carrying.

After an absence of nearly two years, Daniel returned to Rebecca and his family with nothing to show for his long journey except his glowing stories of the beautiful Kentucky land. The loss of the furs was an enormous blow. In the early 1770s, beaver pelts were worth two and a half dollars each, rarer otter skins worth as much as five dollars apiece. Even though common, a deerskin—especially a buckskin—was worth a dollar. Eventually a dollar and a buck would have the same meaning on the frontier.

A hundred or more deerskins could be carried on a single packhorse. The theft of several horses loaded with furs meant a huge loss of income to Daniel and his family. Despite his troubles with the Indians, Daniel could think of little else than moving his family to the meadowlands of Kentucky. But for some time, he would not have the money to buy provisions to make the move.

When Daniel returned home, the Regulation movement in North Carolina was at its height. Although it would be five years before the signing of the Declaration of Independence would formally begin the American Revolution, on the North Carolina frontier settlers were already battling British Redcoats in open warfare.

In May of 1771, the British government sent an army of soldiers to battle the Regulators of North Carolina. The Regulation movement was completely crushed. The Battle of Alamance, as the fight was called, sent the surviving Regulators running. Many of the defeated settlers decided to move westward; some would try to cross the high mountains into Kentucky.

Daniel Boone had never approved of the violence of the Regulators. But he also had had his fill of heavy-handed British rule. He saw Kentucky as a way of escaping both the English government and the advance of civilization in North Carolina.

Again, he talked to his friend, Richard Henderson, the wealthy judge who was interested in buying land in Kentucky. Henderson sent letter after letter to British authorities seeking the right to buy Kentucky land from the Indians. But the answer he so dearly wanted never came. He was not ready to attempt to move without British approval.

For two years, Daniel could think of little other than moving Rebecca and his growing family to Kentucky. But with little money and no backing from Judge Henderson, the trip across the mountains seemed impossible.

To be closer to the wilderness land he loved, he moved his family to Tennessee and roamed the hills on hunting trips, at least twice actually entering the present boundaries of the state of Kentucky. In Tennessee, Daniel met Captain William Russell, a frontier leader among the settlers there. Gradually, the two men reached an agreement to lead a number of families into Kentucky to form a permanent home.

Seeing that his grand dream was about to come true at last, Daniel rushed back to the Yadkin to sell his house and land. But the people who worked for Lord Granville, the man to whom North Carolina had been given by the English king, made the task difficult. Many corrupt officials had to be bribed before the land, legally owned by Daniel, could be sold.

When his land was sold at last, there was yet another delay. In May of 1773, Rebecca gave birth to the couple's sixth child. Rebecca and the new baby were not able to make the difficult journey across the mountains until September.

By the time Daniel was ready to begin the trip, many people were interested in going with him. From the Clinch River in Virginia and Tennessee came many of Captain William Russell's followers. Some of Daniel's old neighbors from the Yadkin valley also decided to join the expedition.

Late in September, 1773, Daniel, Rebecca, and their family led a party of forty settlers from a starting point on the Clinch River toward the Cumberland Gap and Kentucky. Captain Russell and a number of other settlers followed a few miles behind.

As the journey continued, Russell hurried his party to

catch up with the group led by Daniel. Camping just east of the great gap in the mountains, Daniel sent his eldest son James, now seventeen, along the trail to bring Russell's group forward.

James had little difficulty finding the second party. He gave Captain Russell directions to Daniel's camp. With several of Russell's followers, James Boone turned around and hurried to rejoin his father before nightfall.

Darkness came when James was just a couple of miles from his father's camp. Not knowing they were so close to Daniel, James and the people with him decided to build a fire along the trail and spend the night.

Of the six people in James Boone's tiny party, only two, James himself and Captain Russell's son Henry, also seventeen years old, were experienced outdoorsmen. Both young men must have worried as they heard the unusually close howls of wolves that night.

At dawn, their worst fears came to pass. A band of Shawnee warriors attacked the sleeping settlers from all sides. Only two escaped. James Boone and Henry Russell were both struck by arrows. But the worst was not over.

The Shawnee Indians, furious that settlers should try to enter Kentucky when the British king had promised they would not, decided to torture their captives. They began slashing and torturing the young men. The two men who escaped heard the boys scream for mercy.

Finally both boys died. The Shawnee warriors took the guns and other supplies from the little camp and left. One of the settlers who had escaped came out of his hiding place and saw the terrible sight. He ran ahead to Daniel's camp to deliver the horrible news.

At the site of the massacre, the sad parties led by Daniel Boone and William Russell met to bury the first victims of the effort to settle Kentucky. Rebecca found a clean sheet to wrap around the bloody body of her eldest son. Daniel and William Russell dug their graves.

Few of the settlers had any desire to continue across the mountains and into Kentucky. Daniel's dream of life in a paradise called Kentucky had become a nightmare. Their farm on the Yadkin was gone. Now they could only take shelter in the cabin of a friend who lived along the Clinch River, deep in the Allegheny Mountains.

A painting by G. Caleb Bingham showing Daniel Boone leading pioneers into the west in 1775.

Chapter 5

THE WILDERNESS ROAD

Daniel, Rebecca, and their remaining children fled to the mountains of western Virginia to find safety from the angry Indians. But word of the brutal murders swept across the American frontier like wildfire. Never before had children of such famous frontiersmen been killed in such a brutal way.

Before long, settlers and Indians were fighting again, in the Allegheny Mountains and westward. Indians, as well as settlers, were killed. On two occasions, officials from Virginia asked Daniel to travel west, into Indian territory, to collect settlers and bring them to the relative safety of Virginia. Daniel did so without argument, and on one of his trips he visited the grave of his son.

In the meantime, Lord Dunmore, the British governor of the colony of Virginia, was organizing soldiers to fight the Shawnee and Cherokee Indians. When he returned from his second trip across the mountains, Daniel was appointed lieutenant in the Virginia army. He was charged with defending one of the forts along the Clinch River.

News that Daniel was in charge of one of the small forts soon spread to other nearby forts. Everyone along the frontier knew that Daniel Boone, more than any other man, well understood the Indians and could offer the best chance of surviving the wars. Soon, people in other forts were asking Daniel to lead them, too. He accepted the leadership of three different forts, but the Indian war would soon be over.

On October 10, 1774, a force of more than a thousand colonial soldiers defeated a huge army of Shawnee warriors in West Virginia. This was the largest Indian war ever fought east of the Mississippi River, and it became known as Lord Dunmore's War. It probably could have been avoided. But Lord Dunmore, anxious to rid his lands in Virginia of all Indians, refused to listen to their complaints, even though they were often well founded.

Lord Dunmore felt that his war was a great victory, both for himself and the British Crown. But, from Boston to Philadelphia to the American frontier, the fires of revolution were already beginning to burn brightly. The training Dunmore gave the soldiers of Virginia would soon help them drive him out of his colony. Ten months earlier, a group of colonists in Boston disguised as Indians had dumped British tea into Boston Harbor rather than pay a tax on it.

The end of Lord Dunmore's War gave Daniel's old friend Judge Richard Henderson new hope for settling the land of Kentucky. Although his term of office as a judge in North Carolina had ended in 1773, Henderson was still an expert at law. He studied the many claims for the ownership of

Kentucky and decided that the Cherokee Indians were the rightful owners. The time was finally right, he decided, to attempt to buy it from the Indians.

In the fall of 1774, Henderson and a friend met with a number of leaders from the Cherokee nation. The Indians might be willing to sell the land, the Indian chiefs said, but the price would not be cheap. But perhaps goods worth ten thousand British pounds would be enough. Henderson and the Indian leaders agreed to meet again early the next year.

Henderson and Daniel Boone had talked about settling Kentucky for many years. Daniel, Henderson understood, knew about Kentucky and had met many Cherokee leaders. Now that Lord Dunmore's Indian wars were at an end, Daniel was no longer needed in the Virginia army. He agreed to go along with Henderson and others to meet the Cherokee Indians.

Henderson found many other people eager to buy land in Kentucky. Each contributed money to an organization Henderson called the Transylvania Company. The Transylvania Company soon had enough money and supplies to offer the Cherokee the price they had asked for Kentucky. A great Cherokee chief named Attakullaculla traveled to North Carolina to inspect the goods. The chief agreed that the supplies Henderson offered were a fair price for the land.

From North Carolina, Henderson and his followers assembled a small wagon train and headed for the Cherokee lands. From his temporary home on Virginia's Clinch River, Daniel Boone also headed toward the meeting ground. The two parties met at Sycamore Shoals, a holy land of the Cherokee nation on the south shore of the Watauga River, near the present site of Elizabethton, Tennessee.

As Henderson and Boone waited in the little valley of the Watauga River, they saw the tribes of Cherokee begin coming into the valley. Soon, the valley was filled with more than a thousand Indians. There were many chiefs: among them were Savanooka, the Raven; Onistositah, the Corn Tassel; Willanaughwa, the Great Eagle. But the greatest of the chiefs were Oconostota, who was considered the emperor, and Attakullaculla, who had traveled to North Carolina to meet with Henderson. Attakullaculla's son, called Dragging-Canoe, was one of the Cherokee nation's great warriors. His words at the peace meeting would be remembered for years.

Henderson made a point to meet and greet all the Indian chiefs. Daniel already knew many of them and regarded them as friends. While the Indian women built lodges and campfires, the chiefs, warriors, and old men held private meetings. They agreed to try to come to terms with the settlers.

When the time for the great powwow had finally arrived, Henderson began the meeting by asking the Cherokee leaders if the land of Kentucky was actually theirs to sell. The chiefs went back to discuss the question with their tribes. Not until the next day did they report that Kentucky did, indeed, belong to the Cherokee nation. The Iroquois Indians and their friends, sometimes called the Six Nations, had claimed the land, but they never defeated the Cherokee. Kentucky could not be theirs. And the Shawnee had been driven out long ago.

Next, Henderson said that his company would like to buy all the land west of the Allegheny Mountains between the Kentucky River and the Cumberland River. He thought the land amounted to about twenty million acres. In return, he offered "two thousand pounds of lawful money of Great Britain" and the goods Chief Attakullaculla had already seen.

An interpreter put Henderson's words into the Cherokee language and told the chiefs what had been offered. After a long pause, Attakullaculla stood up and said that he would take the offer. One by one, the other chiefs also agreed to sell their land. After each of the chiefs had spoken, Attakullaculla's young son, Dragging-Canoe, arose and gave a much different speech.

Dragging-Canoe said that whole Indian nations had melted away like balls of snow before the sun. The settlers had passed the mountains and settled on Cherokee lands. Now they wanted their actions to be called legal by a treaty. But the settlers would always need more Indian land. The remaining Indians would have to run to some far distant wilderness. There they would be allowed to stay for only a short while, until they again saw the same greedy settlers advancing. When the settlers were unable to point out any further hiding place for the miserable Cherokee, they would bring an end to the entire race. Shouldn't the Cherokee run all risks rather than face their own destruction? These treaties might be all right for men too old to hunt or fight, but he had his young warriors about him. And they would keep their own lands!

The words of young Dragging-Canoe put the chiefs into an uproar. Henderson was shocked by the speech and at once called for a halt in the meeting. He offered the Indians a great feast; and much whiskey, and tried again to become friends. After more discussion, the chiefs finally agreed to the deal. On March 17, 1775, the three most important leaders of the Cherokee nation signed a parchment treaty selling the land of Kentucky to Henderson and his partners.

Despite his great success, there was one more thing that Henderson wanted. "I have more goods, arms, and ammunition that you have not yet seen," Henderson told the Cherokee leaders. "There is land between where we now stand and Kentucky. I do not like to walk over the land of my brothers, and want to buy from them a road to Kentucky."

At hearing these words, Dragging-Canoe became furious. With his finger he pointed westward toward Kentucky, and said, "We have given you this, why do you ask more?" He rose to his feet and stormed away from the meeting. But before he left, he turned directly to Daniel Boone and said, "You have bought a fair land, but there is a cloud hanging over it. You will find its settlement dark and bloody."

Despite Dragging-Canoe's chilling warning, Henderson pressed ahead for the right to build a road from the Cumberland Gap to Kentucky. Eventually, the chiefs agreed to this as well.

As soon as the treaties had been settled, Daniel headed toward the tiny settlement called Long Island, which was deep in the Allegheny Mountains, east of Cumberland Gap. There, he would begin the work of building the Wilderness Road to Kentucky. Once a road was built over the mountains and through the thick forests of eastern Kentucky, it would be much easier for large bands of settlers to move to the land the Transylvania Company had just purchased from the Cherokee Indians.

At Long Island, Daniel got together thirty armed workers, each with a horse. Daniel told the workers that, if they helped to cut down trees and clear a road to Kentucky, each would get free land from the Transylvania Company. Daniel himself would get two thousand acres.

While Rebecca and the family stayed along the Clinch River, Daniel began the enormous task of building a road through the wilderness. The road to the flatlands of Kentucky, some two hundred miles away, crossed some of the most difficult territory imaginable.

Fortunately, over much of the territory to be covered by the Wilderness Road, Daniel and his crew could follow paths used often by Indians and hunters. Following the valleys of Moccasin Creek and then Troublesome Creek, the road-builders widened the trails once used by Cherokee and Shawnee warriors.

Chopping down every tree in their way, the men continued along several more creeks and soon passed over a low spot on Powell Mountain. In the Powell valley, they could see the long white line of the Cumberland Mountains directly ahead of them. Shortly before they reached the great Cumberland Gap, Boone and his workers ran into old Joseph Martin, the man Daniel had met when he was traveling to Kentucky with John Finley.

Martin and his followers had been driven from the Cumberland Mountains by Cherokee Indians shortly after Daniel's first visit. Like many other settlers who had fled eastward to escape Indian attacks, the people with Joseph Martin now felt it was safe to return to their frontier cabins. All were hard at work rebuilding their homes.

From the Martin settlement to the Cumberland Gap, there was little for the roadbuilders to do. The twenty-five-mile-long path had been well worn by herds of buffalo, Indian hunters and warriors, and finally by explorers. As they passed through the great gap in the mountains, Daniel and his crew saw that there would be still more easy going.

Another Indian trail led all the way to the Cumberland River of Kentucky. But at the Cumberland River, the easy road to the flatlands of north-central Kentucky ended. Now the roadbuilders turned north, chopping and slashing their way through forests choked with thick underbrush. The farther north they brought the Wilderness Road, the lower the mountains became.

At last the roadbuilders came to Big Hill and a wide gap in the northernmost range of mountains. Below them were the clover-covered meadows of Kentucky. For two more days Daniel and his workers followed a buffalo trail through the tall grass of the open fields. All the men rejoiced over the land they were passing through.

Game seemed to be everywhere. Great herds of buffalo were spotted several times each day. Tracks of deer, bear, and smaller game could be seen all about them. There were large flocks of wild turkeys. And the open fields and gently rolling hills seemed ideal for farming.

Even to Daniel Boone, the recent warning of Dragging-Canoe seemed like a distant memory. The land seemed gentle beyond imagination on March 24, 1775, when the men made camp in a forest about three miles south of the present site of Richmond, Kentucky.

About an hour before dawn, rifle shots rang out from the

forest. A band of Shawnee warriors completely surprised the exhausted roadbuilders. Daniel, his brother Squire, and the rest of the workers grabbed what they could and scattered into the woods.

In the dark forest, Daniel gradually brought his men together. Together, they were eventually able to drive the Indians away, but the attack had been a costly one. Two men died, and several more were seriously wounded. Daniel sent out scouts to hunt for food and to watch for Indians. The scouts came upon a young boy wandering in the wilderness. The boy reported that another group of settlers, headed by Captain James Harrod, had been attacked by Indians the night before.

Now the roadbuilders feared the worst. Kentucky may have been purchased fairly from the Cherokee Indians, but the Shawnee had not been a part of the treaty. And some wondered how many of the young Cherokee warriors would honor the treaty signed by their fathers.

Daniel knew that the effort to settle Kentucky was at a turning point. On April 1, he sent word of the attack with a messenger headed east to find Richard Henderson. Daniel explained that it was necessary for Henderson to come to Kentucky with reinforcements right away, to combat the alarming Indian attacks. "Now is the time to flusterate their intentions," Daniel said, talking about the Indians on the warpath, "and keep the country whilst we are in it. If we give way to them now, it will ever be the case."

When Richard Henderson got Daniel's message, he knew that the pioneer was right. But Henderson also had another good reason to leave his home. When Lord Dunmore, still the governor of Virginia, learned of the activities of the Transylvania Company, he went into an angry rage. The British governor of North Carolina became so angry that he called for Henderson's arrest.

British rulers in America now had plenty of reason to fear the increasing power of the American colonists. Just eighteen days after Daniel sent his hurried message to Richard Henderson, the first great battle of the American Revolution took place in Concord, Massachusetts. The British had fought hard to make their American colony safe. They were not about to give it up. They regarded people like Richard Henderson as little more than "land pirates."

Henderson and a group of about thirty armed horsemen began following the Wilderness Road Daniel Boone had blazed just a few weeks earlier. As Henderson and his men began the difficult journey across the mountains, Daniel moved his remaining men to a point where the Kentucky River was met by Otter Creek. There they built a small fort.

Henderson arrived at the tiny fort on April 20, 1775, one day after the Battle of Concord had started the American revolutionary war hundreds of miles to the northeast. At once, Henderson began directing the building of a larger fort near the one Boone and his men had put up quickly. The fort would become the capital of the new settlement around it. In honor of Daniel's help, all agreed that the town would be called Boonesborough.

Boonesborough was not the only new town in Kentucky. Nearby were Harrodsburg, Logan Station, and Boiling Spring. The pioneers who came to live in these towns just being born had not yet heard of the American Revolution. For a while, their thoughts would turn only to the growing of crops, the hunting of game, and protection from Indians. But soon enough, all would become part of the struggle to give birth to a new nation.

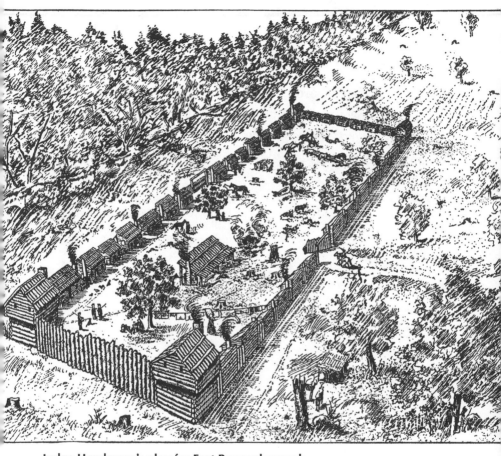

Judge Henderson's plan for Fort Boonesborough

Left: Daniel Boone wore pants and shirts made of buckskin and moccasins of deerskin.

Below: On July 14, 1776, Jemima Boone and Betsy and Frances Callaway were captured by Indians.

Squire Boone, Daniel's father

Daniel Boone is captured by Indians.

An engraving of Daniel Boone by J.B. Longacre from
the original painting by Chester Harding about 1835.

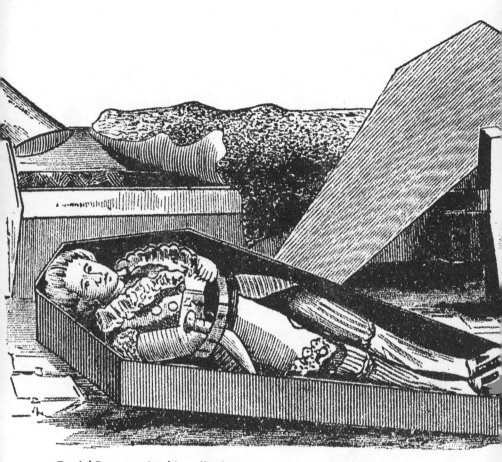

Daniel Boone trying his coffin for size

Although Daniel Boone was born in Pennsylvania and died in Missouri, he opened the way west for American settlers when he made a trail through the Cumberland Gap and established Boonesborough, Kentucky. He is buried in Frankfort, Kentucky.

Above: The log cabin built by Daniel Boone in St. Charles County, Missouri. Below: The Nathan Boone House in Defiance, Missouri was built somewhere between 1815 and 1820.

Chapter 6

THE LONG HANDSHAKE

By June, 1775, the fort at Boonesborough was becoming a major structure. Twenty-three cabins were built in a large rectangular pattern, their outer walls giving protection against Indian attacks. Inside the rectangle were three more log cabins. One of the cabins was used as a gunsmith shop by Daniel's brother Squire.

As soon as Henderson arrived at the new fort near the Kentucky River, he had taken over command of the settlement from Daniel Boone. But most of the settlers still thought Daniel was their real leader.

Henderson had little experience living in the wilderness. He had even less understanding of how to hunt game for food. With Henderson's approval, hunters left Boonesborough to seek buffalo. When they found vast herds, they slaughtered many more than they could use, leaving most to rot on the ground. In a matter of weeks, all the great herds that the roadbuilders had first seen in the flatlands of Kentucky had been driven away.

Daniel knew that such hunting methods were unwise and would soon lead to a shortage of meat. Before he traveled east in June to bring Rebecca and his family to Boonesborough, Daniel helped to make one of the settlement's first laws. The law set limits on the amount of game each hunter could take.

In the meantime, Richard Henderson was interested in making the land of Kentucky, which he called Transylvania, the fourteenth colony in America. His timing was awful. Already, the Continental Congress was meeting in Philadelphia. Although men like George Washington and Thomas Jefferson were still saying they were loyal to the British Crown, the earliest steps toward the Declaration of Independence were already being taken.

Traveling east, Henderson tried to get Transylvania recognized by British officials as well as the Continental Congress. He failed on both counts. Eventually, Transylvania would be forgotten. During the early years of the revolutionary war, Virginia would take over the land once called Transylvania, calling it the County of Kentucky. Richard Henderson would move on to Tennessee, where he would help to make a settlement that was later called Nashville.

On September 8, 1775, Daniel brought Rebecca and his family into Boonesborough for the first time. As always, other people followed him into the wilderness. This time, his party included at least twenty-one men of fighting age. But for the roadbuilders turned fort builders now living in Boonesborough, the sight of women and children arriving at last must have been a welcome one.

With Richard Henderson gone, Daniel took full control of Boonesborough. Under his careful leadership, all the settlers felt safe. Soon, more pioneers arrived at Boonesborough and the neighboring settlements, including women and children. By the end of fall, nearly five hundred people lived in the little fortress along the Kentucky River.

As the colonists along the Atlantic Coast were getting ready for all-out war with England, Daniel Boone was directing efforts to strengthen his frontier fort against Indian attacks. Although there were signs that Indians were traveling around the land outside of the fort, there had been no serious problems since the winter before.

On July 14, 1776, ten days after the Declaration of Independence was signed in Philadelphia, there were few indications of war around Boonesborough and the other frontier forts. It was Sunday, a time for prayers and relaxation. Under the warm summer sun, Daniel's teenaged daughter Jemima and two daughters of another settler named Richard Callaway had taken a canoe across the river to pick flowers.

On the far shore of the river, the girls were surprised and captured by a band of Shawnee Indians, one of whom recognized Jemima as the daughter of the man they called "Wide-Mouth." Jemima had listened well to her father's tales of the Indians. She knew it was against Shawnee beliefs to harm female captives and that she and her friends would not be hurt.

So she made every effort to slow the Indians' retreat away from Boonesborough. Along the way, she left torn pieces of her skirt, and then broken twigs, to mark her path. Back at Boonesborough, Daniel learned that the canoe taken by the girls had been seen adrift at the far side of the river. He understood immediately what had happened.

Without bothering to put on his moccasins, he rushed to the bank of the river. Richard Callaway, the father of the other two captured girls, was anxious to ride after them as soon as the men had crossed the river. But Daniel had another plan. He sent Callaway with some horsemen north, where they could cut off the Indians at a necessary river crossing. Daniel and some others set off on foot following Jemima's trail of torn cloth.

Before they had gone many miles, it grew dark. Daniel and his group made a makeshift camp. Daniel sent one of the young men back to Boonesborough to get rifles, gunpowder, and his moccasins.

Jemima used every excuse to slow down the Indians who held her captive. Her delays allowed Daniel and his rescue party to overtake the Indians the next day, before they had gotten to the big river crossing. But as soon as the settlers saw the Shawnee warriors, one of the men fired his gun. Now the girls' lives were in danger.

Daniel and another man quickly shot two of the Indians, but there was no time to reload their long rifles. The settlers jumped up and rushed into the Indian camp, grabbing the girls and retreating into the thick woods.

When Daniel and his rescue party brought the three girls unharmed back into Boonesborough, everyone cheered. But they did not cheer when Richard Callaway and the other riders returned somewhat later. Why had they not captured the Indians who had kidnapped the girls? Surely, the Shawnee would have had to cross the river where Callaway and the other men were waiting. To himself, Callaway blamed Daniel for making him look like a fool. He would hold the grudge for a long time.

The others in Boonesborough soon forgot the excitement of the kidnapping. A month or two later, a traveler from Virginia brought a newspaper that reported the signing of the Declaration of Independence. As the stirring words were read aloud, many of the Boonesborough settlers shouted with joy.

Daniel, too, was moved by the words of the Declaration of Independence, but he had other worries. He knew that, to the east, the battles of the revolutionary war would be raging. He also knew that the British had learned, during the French and Indian War, how to make friends with the Indians and turn them against the settlers.

In the British fort at Detroit, far to the north, the British governor Henry Hamilton was offering rewards to any Indian who could bring in the scalp of an American. His plan was perfectly clear to Daniel. By destroying the settlements in the western frontier, British soldiers would be able to attack the armies from the thirteen colonies, now called the United States of America, from the west.

Seventeen-seventy-seven would be a difficult year for everyone on the American frontier. Then, the settlers called it the "Year of the Bloody Sevens." In the first months, a number of hunters passing the Boonesborough fort were killed by Indians. A few weeks later, Daniel's brother Squire was attacked just outside the walls of the fort. He managed to escape, but a tomahawk blow to his face left a scar that lasted the rest of his life.

In April, men gathering firewood outside the walled town were attacked by six Indians. Daniel led a group of ten riflemen through the gates of the fort and began chasing the attackers. It was a terrible mistake of judgment.

Just out of sight stood the Shawnee chief Black Fish with a huge band of Shawnee warriors. As Daniel and the other riflemen charged away from the fort, Black Fish and his warriors swarmed in from the woods, coming between the fortress walls and the defenders. They were trapped.

Daniel and his men shot at the Indians facing them. But there would be no time to reload their rifles. So Daniel led the riflemen in a charge for the fort, fighting the Indians standing between them and the safety of the walled town. Before Daniel made it back into the gate, he was shot in the foot. Jemima Boone helped her wounded father into the fort as riflemen fired at the Indians for cover.

Daniel's wound took several months to heal. During that time, he directed the defense of Boonesborough from his sickbed. There were other attacks by the Shawnee, but somehow the riflemen managed to keep them out of the fort. But travel outside the walls of Boonesborough was so dangerous that few men attempted to hunt for food or even get water from the nearby river.

The Virginia army, because of the fort's important position defending against Indian and British attack from the west, sent forty soldiers to Boonesborough in late summer. Even with reinforcements, it was difficult to hunt for food and gather water. Before the crops planted around the tiny fort could be harvested, the Indians burned them. When winter struck, it was colder than anyone could remember.

All of the settlers were glad to see the "Year of the Bloody Sevens" come to an end. They did not know that the following year, 1778, would be even worse.

In the early winter of the new year, Daniel led thirty riflemen out of Boonesborough to gather salt at the Licking River, about forty miles north of the fort. When they reached the salt-rich river, the men began their work, boiling water in huge kettles until only salt remained at the bottom. While they worked, Daniel rode a horse in a wide circle around them, always looking out for Indians. In a blinding snowstorm, he was surprised by a small band of Shawnee.

Daniel knew that he would not be able to reload his long rifle quickly enough to shoot all the Indians. His only choice was to give up. The Indians captured him and returned to their chief.

When Daniel arrived at the Indian camp, he couldn't believe his eyes. There, with at least a hundred Indian warriors, was the great chief Black Fish. Worse yet, camping with the Shawnee were a number of British soldiers! Clearly, this was not an ordinary war party. The British soldiers would do everything they could to talk the Indians into a final attack on the Boonesborough fort.

Many of the Indians recognized Daniel, and he remembered many of them. One of the Shawnee, named Captain Will, had stolen Daniel's horse during his first trip to Kentucky.

"Hello, Captain Will," Daniel said, trying to sound cheerful. "Have you enjoyed my horse? Or did it run away, like me?"

"You will not run away this time, Wide-Mouth," Captain Will replied. Daniel and the Shawnee kept joking. Even Black Fish found the conversation funny. But Daniel knew there was nothing funny about his situation.

He thought of the people left behind at Boonesborough,

mostly women and children. Then he made a desperate decision. He would tell Black Fish about the armed salt makers working on the Licking River. With so many captives, perhaps Black Fish would be happy to take them back to his Shawnee capital north of the Ohio River. Perhaps Boonesborough could be saved.

With a dozen rifles pointed at his back, Daniel led the Indians to the spot on the Licking River where the salt makers were working. Vastly outnumbered and completely surprised, all were forced to surrender. Then Black Fish and his advisers held a meeting. Although the Indians spoke in Shawnee, Daniel understood enough to know that they were in trouble.

The Indians had promised not to kill the men from Boonesborough if Daniel led the way to them. But many of the warriors argued that the settlers had often broken their word, so why should the Indians keep theirs? Daniel gave a speech, asking for mercy for his brothers. Then a vote was taken. Amazingly, Daniel himself was allowed to vote.

Black Fish had become friends with Daniel, as had many other Indians. The son of this great Shawnee chief had been one of the Indians who kidnapped Daniel's daughter and the two Callaway girls from Boonesborough, and he had been killed in the fighting that followed. Although Daniel was forty-three years old, the chief had decided to adopt him, to replace the son he had lost.

The Indians passed a brightly painted wooden war club. Throwing it to the ground meant death to the settlers. Passing it to the next warrior meant life. When the voting was done, the Shawnee had elected to let the settlers live—by a difference of two votes, Daniel's being one of them.

Black Fish led the prisoners to his village, largest of the Shawnee, called Little Chillicothe. The British soldiers traveling with the Indians were enraged. They had demanded that Black Fish go on to capture Boonesborough, but they were ignored. At Little Chillicothe, it was decided to march the prisoners to Detroit, where the British governor, Henry Hamilton, would buy them from the Shawnee.

Black Fish decided to take Daniel to Detroit also, but he was not going to sell him to the British soldiers. Instead, he would show Governor Hamilton how his brave warriors had captured the most famous man on the American frontier.

At Detroit, Governor Hamilton treated Daniel with great respect. He, too, had heard many stories about the famous outdoorsman. Hamilton offered Black Fish a small fortune in silver for Daniel, but Black Fish refused to give up his adopted son. The other men from Boonesborough were put into a British prison.

It was late spring before Black Fish, his adopted son Daniel, and the rest of the Shawnee warriors returned to the Indian village of Little Chillicothe. On the journey south from Detroit, Black Fish stopped at many Shawnee villages.

At each, he announced that the Shawnee would soon attack Boonesborough, and that their warriors must be ready.

Daniel knew that he had to warn the people at the fort. But how could he escape? Everywhere he went, the Indians kept a careful eye on him. During the early months of summer, Daniel lived with his adopted family. Even Black Fish's wife liked her new son. In a few weeks, Daniel was allowed to use a rifle to hunt small game close to the village. But always, he was closely watched.

Finally, the opportunity came. While a Shawnee hunting party was busy shooting at a flock of wild turkeys, Daniel made his escape. He was more than 150 miles from Boonesborough, and without a horse. He had to run to reach the fort in time to give warning of the coming Indian attack.

It took him only four days to cover the great distance on foot. But when he arrived at Boonesborough on the afternoon of June 20, 1778, there was disappointing news. When the salt makers had been taken away by Black Fish, the other settlers thought that they must have been killed. So Rebecca and the rest of Daniel's family, except his daughter Jemima and his brother Squire, had gone back to North Carolina. Daniel took command of the fort soon after he arrived. He strengthened the walls around the outside, replacing wood that was rotting. He sent messages to nearby forts, asking for reinforcements. About two dozen came. And he sent messengers eastward, hoping to find soldiers from Virginia and North Carolina willing to help in the defense of Boonesborough.

Black Fish and his huge army of Indians arrived at Boonesborough on September 7, 1778. Besides Black Fish's Shawnee warriors, there were Cherokee, Wyandot, and Mingo braves as well. There were also British soldiers dressed in their bright red uniforms, and even French soldiers from Canada.

Daniel knew that the fifty or so fighting men in Boonesborough were hopelessly outnumbered. Black Fish himself walked up to the gate and called for his adopted son. Showing no fear, Daniel came out of the fort to meet his Indian father.

The two men talked for some time. Black Fish explained that his warriors were hungry. Daniel said that they should take what they needed of the grain growing outside the walls, and the cattle grazing there as well. He knew there was no way to stop them.

Black Fish then said that he had come to capture Boonesborough, and showed Daniel a letter from Governor Hamilton of Detroit. The letter said that if the Boonesborough settlers would surrender, the Indians would treat them well. Otherwise, there would be terrible death and destruction.

When Daniel said that his people would not give up, Black Fish looked disappointed. He had hoped to avoid a battle. For two more days, the Indians and settlers held meetings just outside the gates of the fort. Each time, the Indians demanded a surrender, and Boone and his men stalled for time. Perhaps soon, Daniel kept thinking, reinforcements would arrive.

On the third day, September 9, Boone realized that he could stall no longer. He told Black Fish that the settlers could never give up Boonesborough without a fight. Then Black Fish said something amazing. Rather than begin a battle in which many would die, it would be better to sign a peace treaty.

Daniel found such an astonishing offer hard to believe, but he could not refuse the chance for peace. Black Fish told Daniel to send nine men from Boonesborough to meet the various Indian chiefs the next day, and a lasting treaty would be signed. Daniel suggested a spot for the signing that was within rifle range of the fort. He was still suspicious of the surprising offer from Black Fish.

That night the Indians prepared a great feast, which they offered to many of the people inside the fort. Although there was hardly any food at all inside Boonesborough, Daniel directed that a feast be offered to the Indians, too.

The next day, Daniel and seven other leaders from Boonesborough walked out of the gate to meet the Indian chiefs. Black Fish had asked for nine men, but Daniel felt he could not spare the last riflemen. All who were left were stationed along the walls of Boonesborough, with their rifles pointed at the gathering group of treaty makers.

Daniel was surprised to see that his eight-man party was met by a group of eighteen Indians. When he asked why, Black Fish said that eighteen Indian villages had sent warriors.

Then Black Fish said that since the settlers had purchased Kentucky from the Cherokee, they should be allowed to stay in peace. Black Fish asked that they sign a paper in which they promised to obey the orders of the British government. Faced by such a huge army of warriors, Daniel and the other men gladly signed.

Black Fish began passing a peace pipe around to both Indians and settlers. Finally, he announced, all that was needed was for everyone to shake hands, and then the Indians would go in peace. However, Black Fish continued, since there were twice as many Indians as settlers at the meeting, each settler would shake hands with two Indians.

Black Fish walked directly to Daniel Boone and grabbed his arm firmly with both hands. A second Indian took Daniel's other arm in his hands. In much the same way, two Indians took the hands of each settler present at the meeting. Now, each of the best riflemen from Boonesborough was firmly in the grasp of two Indian braves. The Indians smiled broadly as "the long handshake" continued.

Did it mean peace at last, or was it a trap?

Chapter 7

THE BATTLE OF BOONESBOROUGH

It may never be known for sure whether or not the Indians holding Daniel Boone's arms and the arms of the other settlers were acting in good faith. As the Indians' grips tightened, shots rang out from the Boonesborough fort. At almost the same instant, some of the warriors in the huge army outside Boonesborough also began shooting.

Daniel and the other men from the fort broke loose from the Indians holding them and immediately began running toward the fort. Daniel's brother Squire was shot and fell to the ground, but he got back to his feet and joined the others racing for the gate. Remarkably, every one of the men made it inside. The Battle of Boonesborough had begun on September 10, 1778.

Although Daniel and Squire had made it to the safety of the fort, both were wounded. Squire had been shot in the shoulder; Daniel had been badly cut by a tomahawk in the head and back. But there was no time to take care of their wounds. The huge army, in which Daniel had counted 444 Indians, was now attacking the fort from all sides, especially the north wall.

With women and children standing behind the riflemen to

reload their guns, the men inside Boonesborough drove the attacking army away. As night came, Jemima bandaged Daniel's wounds. Then her father walked around the fort, talking to the wounded, including his brother Squire.

Sleep came hard for the defenders of Boonesborough. Many must have feared that the next day would be their last. But when morning came, the people inside the fort watched the Indian army break camp, ride their horses across the Kentucky River, and head away in the distance.

Daniel now figured that Black Fish had fooled him once. He was determined not to be taken in a second time. He allowed no one to leave the gates of the fort. Instead he prepared for a second attack, cleaning rifles again and again, and doing whatever was possible to make the walls around the fort more secure.

In just a few hours, the Indians returned, attacking the fort with everything they had. They had not tricked the settlers into leaving the protection of the fort. Now they seemed to be attacking with even greater fury. The bullets struck the outer walls so often they sounded like a continuous drumroll.

Inside, it was barely possible for the defenders to peer over the walls without being shot in the head. But when one of the men in the fort managed to catch a glimpse of the river, he saw a strange sight. The once clear water was now filled with mud.

The Indians were digging a tunnel from the shore of the Kentucky River directly toward Boonesborough. Daniel knew that if the tunnel were completed, Indians would be able to enter the fort without being fired upon. Black Fish was once again trying to trick the settlers. The chief had hoped that no one in the fort would notice the tunnel digging during the fearsome attack.

Daniel was uncertain about how to stop the tunnel makers. Because they worked from the low banks of the river, it was impossible to shoot them from the fort. But the farther they dug, Daniel knew, the closer they came to the interior of Boonesborough.

Finally he thought of a plan. He ordered some of his men to begin digging another tunnel, this one at a right angle to the one Black Fish and his warriors were making. Perhaps it would be possible to make the Indian tunnel collapse. With a tunnel of their own, some of the men from the fort could at least wait underground, ready to attack the Indians before they got out of the tunnels.

On both sides of Boonesborough's walls, the settlers and the Indians worked in the summer heat digging and digging. It would take many days to complete either of the tunnels, but in the meantime there were other dangers. Several times, the Indians set fire to the outer walls of the fort. The men inside were able to put out the flames, but now water was running dangerously low.

Fruit and vegetables were completely gone. The small herd of cattle roaming inside the walls of the fort had no feed and was starving. Each day, a few animals would be killed by stray bullets, but there was little meat on the skinny carcasses. Always, the settlers looked over the walls of the fort, hoping to catch a glimpse of help riding their way. But none came.

On the sixth day of the battle, the men digging the tunnel under the fort could hear the sounds of the Indians digging their tunnel. It was not possible to tell how close they were, but most of the men feared the worst. However, that night brought a more immediate danger.

After a fierce volley of rifle shots, the Indians made an all-out fire attack against Boonesborough. Soon, all the water remaining in the fort had been used to put out the fires. Still more burning arrows struck the outer walls and the roofs of the buildings inside. Now there were several sections of Boonesborough going up in flames, and there was no water left to put them out.

Daniel led all the men, women, and children of Boonesborough into a single cabin, ready to take a final stand against the Indians who would soon be inside the fort. No one had to be told what would happen as soon as the blazing fires destroyed the settlement's outer walls.

But minutes before the flames destroyed the walls of Boonesborough, rain began to fall. The fires went out. And the rain continued. It rained all night and all the next day. Soon, basins put out to catch the rainfall were filling up with life-giving water. The rain continued for a second day and part of the next night.

When dawn came the third morning after the rain had begun, the Indians were gone. Lookouts posted high on the walls saw why the Indian army had given up. The great rainfall of the past days and nights had softened the ground above the Indian tunnel and it had finally collapsed. Now it was nothing but a large ditch, stretching from the bank of the river nearly to the wall of the fort. The Battle of Boonesborough had been won by the people of Boonesborough. In *The Discovery, Settlement and Present State of Kentucke*, author John Finley had Daniel say the following words about the great battle:

> During this dreadful siege, which threatened death in every form, we had two men killed, and four wounded, besides a number of cattle. We killed of the enemy thirty-seven, and wounded a great number. After they were gone, we picked up one hundred and twenty-five pounds weight of bullets, besides what stuck in the logs of our fort.

The Battle of Boonesborough was an important event in the American revolutionary war. Had Boonesborough fallen,

Indians and British troops would have been able to control Kentucky. Instead, the forts along the Kentucky frontier would soon serve as home base for the American armies under George Rogers Clark, who would eventually defeat British forces in the Northwest Territories.

With the battle won, it should have been a time for great rejoicing at Boonesborough. Instead, there would be yet another difficulty for Daniel. Richard Callaway, the man whose daughters had been kidnapped by Indians along with Daniel's daughter Jemima, had held a grudge against the leader of Boonesborough for many months.

Now that the fighting was done, Callaway began to say that it had all been Daniel's fault. Callaway charged that Daniel had led Black Fish and his warriors to the salt makers' camp on the Licking River and that he had made the workers give up. He also said that Daniel started the entire battle by bringing seven other men from the fort outside to meet with Black Fish for "the long handshake." Daniel, Callaway said, seemed to like the British better than his countrymen.

It was decided to hold a court-martial, a trial by military law. (Daniel was still an officer in the Virginia army.) If Daniel was proved guilty of the charges, he could be put in prison or even shot. But the charges were ridiculous, and almost everyone except Richard Callaway seemed to know it.

At the trial, Daniel patiently explained all the events of

the last months, and his reasons for behaving as he did. When the trial was over, he was cleared of all the charges against him. People realized, even more than before, that they owed their lives to Daniel's brave actions. He was promoted to the rank of major.

With the court-martial over, Daniel was finally free to travel back to the Yadkin River to find Rebecca and his family. When he arrived in North Carolina, there were more difficulties.

Many of his old neighbors from the Yadkin valley were Tories, people who sided with the British government during the American Revolution. The Bryans, Rebecca's family, were among those who felt that America should not be at war with Great Britain. It took Daniel many months to convince his wife to return with him to Kentucky.

It is easy to understand why Rebecca did not look forward to going back to Boonesborough. Although the army of George Rogers Clark was having some success against the Indians and British soldiers along the frontier, Indian wars were still raging in Kentucky and northward. There were many tales of terrible fights to the west, and there would be more to come.

Nevertheless, the defense of Boonesborough and the successes of George Rogers Clark were enough to give people the courage to head west in search of game and new land, even while the revolutionary war was raging. A large party of settlers, some of them soldiers, set out with the Boones to follow the Wilderness Road into Kentucky. Among the travelers were Edward and Samuel Boone, Daniel's brothers, and his old friend Abraham Lincoln, grandfather of the famous president.

Daniel and his family arrived in Boonesborough in the fall of 1779. Much had changed since he had left the year before. Richard Callaway, the man who had instigated the court-martial, was now in charge. Daniel certainly could have taken command away from Callaway, but he had no interest in politics. Instead, he left the town named in his honor and built a cabin a few miles west.

Although he no longer lived in Boonesborough, most of the settlers in and around the fort still thought of Daniel as their natural leader. Early in 1780, news arrived that the land titles of the old Transylvania Company had been nullified by the government of Virginia. It meant that none of the Boonesborough residents legally owned the land they had fought so hard to defend.

Settlers along the Kentucky River raised almost $50,000 in cash to buy new land titles. They gave it all to Daniel, who started eastward to buy new land deeds. But while he was sleeping in a small inn in Virginia, all the money was stolen.

Daniel must have believed that he carried the most sorrowful news of the frontier as he returned, empty-handed, across the Cumberland Gap and traveled down the Wilderness Road to the settlements along the Kentucky River. But when he arrived, he would learn that there was worse news yet.

Indian attacks along the Kentucky frontier had started up again, more savage than ever before. In one of the raids, Richard Callaway was killed. By summer, four forts along the Kentucky frontier were overrun by Indians directed by British commanders. Boonesborough was the largest settlement in western Kentucky still under control of American settlers.

Boonesborough would not fall. The army of George Rogers Clark rushed south and attacked the villages of a number of Indian tribes who only recently had been taking over forts. But smaller isolated battles continued.

Five years earlier, the Cherokee warrior Dragging-Canoe had warned Daniel that Kentucky would become a "dark and bloody" ground. Now, more than ever, his words were becoming frighteningly true. Under Clark's command, every able-bodied pioneer in Kentucky soon became a warrior. Battles with Indians and their British commanders occurred everywhere. Daniel's brother Edward was killed and scalped early in 1780. Later in the war, Daniel's second son, Israel, would suffer the same fate.

Late in 1781, news arrived on the Kentucky frontier that the forces of George Washington had defeated the last great British army in the east. For the Americans in the fast-growing cities along the Atlantic Coast, the revolutionary war was over. But in Kentucky, the fighting went on.

Although he had always named many Indians among his friends, Daniel did his best to defend his countrymen from their attacks. He would seldom be away from the fighting for long.

Earlier in 1781, he had been sent to Richmond, Virginia, to represent his area of Kentucky in the Virginia state legislature. Daniel went to meetings along with such famous patriots as Patrick Henry and Thomas Jefferson. Despite the exciting company he kept, by the next spring he was back fighting Indians in Kentucky.

In 1782, while people along the Eastern seacoast were celebrating the end of the revolutionary war, battles continued along the frontier. Early in the fall, news reached Boonesborough about an Indian attack to the north. Bryan's Station, a town built by Rebecca's family, had been surrounded by Wyandot Indians.

Daniel organized a group from Boonesborough and the men rode north to help defend Bryan's Station. By the time they got there, the Wyandot had gone, after burning all the crops and killing the cattle. Men from other settlements soon arrived, and before long nearly two hundred had gathered together. With such a strong force, it was decided to chase after the retreating Indians.

Along the way, Daniel was surprised to see the clear trail

left by the Wyandot. Usually, Indians would break into small groups after an attack, making their trail much more difficult to follow. This trail, Daniel would later say, could have been followed by a blind man. It went northwest to the Licking River, not far from the place where the Boonesborough salt makers had been taken by Black Fish.

After camping for the night, the troops from Bryan's Station continued along the trail, reaching the Licking River in the early morning. There, they saw the last of the Wyandots scrambling over the far shore. The land beyond the river could not be seen.

Daniel told the others that the Indians might well be hiding just across the river. It made no sense, he argued, to rush into an ambush. Unfortunately, the other leaders did not agree. Against Daniel's advice, the riders charged across the Licking River and rode up the opposite bank. In an instant, the Indians, hidden in little valleys and tiny streambeds, were upon them.

The brief fight that followed was called the Battle of Blue Licks. It was the last great battle of the American revolutionary war, but it was not a victory for the troops from Kentucky. Surprised and badly outnumbered, nearly half of them were killed. Daniel's son Israel was one of them. Carrying his dead son in his arms, Daniel guided his troops back across the Licking River.

Surprisingly, the Indians would never again mount a

major attack in Kentucky. The next year, George Rogers Clark would lead strong assaults against the remaining Indian villages north of the Ohio River. The French, the British, and finally the Indians had been forced to surrender the land of Kentucky to the settlers.

But the "dark and bloody" ground had taken a heavy toll. In it, Daniel had buried two sons, a brother, and dozens of friends. He would never again be able to think of it as paradise.

Chapter 8

FOREVER WESTWARD

The story of Daniel Boone's life after the American Revolution is as strange as anything that can be imagined. In 1784, John Finley's book, *The Discovery, Settlement and Present State of Kentucke*, was published. A long chapter in the book was called "The Adventures of Col. Daniel Boon," which, except for the misspelling of Daniel's last name, contained a fairly accurate story of Daniel's adventures in Kentucky. Daniel himself had told Finley many of the stories.

The book also contained a large map of Kentucky. The map showed the rivers and streams of the land, the major settlements, and even many of the Indian trails. It also showed, of course, the famous Wilderness Road, which Finley labeled "The Road from the old settlements through the great Wilderness."

It quickly became the most popular travel book of its time, and it made Daniel Boone even more famous. Soon, more writers were telling his story, often with little regard for the truth. Before his death in 1820, hundreds of books, poems, stories, and plays would have been written about him, some by such famous authors as Lord Byron and, just slightly later, James Fenimore Cooper.

By his fiftieth birthday in November, 1784, Daniel Boone had become a living legend. But while much of the world began to sing his praises, he lived a simple life on the frontier, often facing many problems. His greatest problem of all was proving that he owned any land at all in Kentucky.

More than any other man, Daniel had opened up the land of Kentucky and made it possible for settlers to move there. He had cleared the land with his own hands, built the first road to it, and defended it against attackers. He had learned how to measure and mark out his own property, and had helped hundreds of other people do the same.

But in the years following the American Revolution, he found it impossible to keep any of the land he had fought so hard to win. The rush to Kentucky was on. By the thousands, settlers passed through the Cumberland Gap and followed the Wilderness Road into central Kentucky. With them came lawyers. Always, the lawyers would find something wrong with Daniel's written claims to his property. And bit by bit, they would take away his land.

Daniel, Rebecca, and the children still living at home moved several times, once to a spot near the site of the famous Battle of Blue Licks. All the while, lawyers were reading his land titles and finding ways to beat them. Hardly a month would go by in which Daniel would not be called into court to defend his land claims against those who would take them away.

Daniel had no formal education. His greatest skill was as a hunter and an explorer. But the Kentucky wilderness was quickly disappearing and with it the game that he was so skilled in hunting. Daniel was deep in debt, with his land holdings shrinking almost daily, and there seemed to be few opportunities open to him.

But an amazing opportunity did come to Daniel, now in his sixties. As always, it called him to move west. The land west of the Mississippi River was not a part of the United States of America. In the 1790s much of it was claimed by the king of Spain. The assistant governor of the Spanish land, a man named Don Zenon Trudeau, had heard many of the great tales about Daniel.

In 1795 one of Daniel's sons had traveled to Missouri and visited with Trudeau. The son returned to his father filled with stories about the land west of the Mississippi River, where game was plentiful and taxes small.

At almost the same time, Trudeau began sending letters directly to Daniel. He invited the old pioneer to move to Missouri, offering to give him much land and give additional land to every member of the Boone family who wanted to come along.

Daniel still had hoped that he could find a comfortable life in Kentucky. But for the next four years, he continued to be hounded by tax collectors and by people intent on taking away his land. By 1799 he could stand it no longer. Now nearly sixty-five, he chopped down an enormous tree and built from it a canoe sixty feet long.

He gave his small remaining amount of land to a relative. He loaded his family and supplies into his enormous canoe. As always, many relatives and friends joined Daniel in his new move to the west.

With Daniel's family in the lead canoe, a parade of boats began moving downstream on the wide Ohio River. But Daniel did not ride in a boat. Instead, he walked along the shore, and would travel this way all along the route to Missouri.

Following the Ohio River to the Mississippi, he passed a number of settlers who recognized the old pioneer.

"Where are you headed to, Daniel?" they would shout. "Why are you leaving?"

"Headin' west," he would answer. "Too crowded here. I want more elbow room."

When the parade of boats reached the Mississippi River, Daniel led them northward to the tiny French settlement called St. Louis. The soldiers at St. Louis held a special celebration in honor of Daniel Boone.

Although most of the people in St. Louis were French, a Spanish flag flew above the town. It signaled that all the land west of the great Mississippi River was owned by Spain. Once again, Daniel Boone and his family would be living in an American land claimed by a European nation.

Daniel and his relatives, especially the Bryans, settled down along the Missouri River about sixty miles west of the Mississippi, near a tiny river called Femme Osage Creek, which flowed into the Missouri. Here, Daniel found happiness once again.

Spanish officials were honored to have the famous old pioneer living among them. In the year 1800, he was made a *syndic*, a kind of judge for the huge Femme Osage district. For four years, Daniel held his court under a huge tree that came to be known as the Judgment Tree. There, he settled the fights and arguments that always seemed to crop up.

Daniel might have gone on this way for the remainder of his days. But once again, the great forces of history were about to overtake him. In the early 1800s, the French emperor Napoleon forced the Spanish king to give all the land west of the Mississippi River in the New World to the French. In 1802 United States President Thomas Jefferson purchased the great land, known as Louisiana, from Napoleon's government.

Suddenly, Daniel Boone discovered that he was, once again, on United States land. It would soon mean trouble.

Daniel had always thought of himself as a hunter, not a farmer. In his old age, he had not bothered to plant crops. Even though the Spanish officials in Missouri had given him 840 acres of land, the fact that he had not farmed it caused problems with the United States government.

American officials were willing to give land titles to people who farmed their land when it was owned by Spain. Daniel had not farmed his land, the officials noted, and therefore he could not own it. As incredible as it may seem, Daniel once again lost his land.

Since he was not a lawyer, Daniel could no longer be a judge under the American government in Missouri. Although the land was no longer his, no one seemed to expect him to leave it. The Louisiana Purchase had doubled the size of America. Unlike the days when he lived in Kentucky, now there seemed to be plenty of land for all.

Daniel and Rebecca went on living in a little cabin near Femme Osage Creek on the Missouri River. Quietly, Daniel continued to hunt and make a small profit from the skins and furs he collected. With a relative, he also started a salt-making business at a nearby lick.

The last years of Daniel's life were filled with great joy and sadness. In 1813, while making maple syrup with her daughter Jemima, Rebecca Boone fell sick and died a few days later. She was about seventy-four years old. In his sorrow, Daniel spent weeks by himself, sitting alone in the fields around his home with his long rifle cradled in his arms.

Now nearly eighty, he began to tell his friends and relatives that perhaps his time had come as well. But he was wrong. Several great adventures lay ahead for the amazing old pioneer.

Soon after Rebecca died, Daniel went to live with his son Nathan, who had built what many said was the first stone house in Missouri. The following year, Congress passed a special law officially giving back Daniel's land in Missouri. The new law called Daniel "the man who has opened the way for millions of his fellow men." President James Madison signed the new law in February, 1814.

Eventually, Daniel would have to sell even the land given him by Congress to pay off old debts from his days in Kentucky. But by now, the little pieces of paper that others fought over to see who owned what meant little to him. For there was yet another adventure ahead.

When he was eighty-two years old, Daniel decided to see the rest of the great American continent. On foot, he began traveling west, across Missouri and the plains of Kansas. He walked across the flatlands and hills of the Dakotas and kept right on going, until he reached the Rocky Mountains. He finally arrived at the present site of Yellowstone National Park. There he spent the winter, hunting and trapping game. The following spring, he walked back to Missouri.

Now, he began to feel that his days of great wandering would have to come to an end. Arthritis was beginning to bother him a bit and he wasn't quite as strong as he used to be.

But the following year he felt sturdy enough to make the comparatively easy trip back to Kentucky. There, he searched for everyone to whom he might yet owe money and paid them back. When he was finished, the old story goes, he had fifty cents to his name. But it made him feel good to know that all his debts had been repaid.

By 1818 he was back at Nathan's home on the Missouri River. During the summer of 1819, a painter named Chester Harding came west to see the old pioneer. He was not the first painter to visit Daniel. A few years earlier, a young man named James Audubon had painted Daniel's portrait.

Now another painter was traveling to see the aged woodsman. He had difficulty finding anyone who knew exactly where Daniel lived. When Harding finally found him, he explained his problems and asked Daniel if he had ever been lost.

"No, I never got lost," Daniel answered after some thought, "but I was bewildered once for three days."

For Daniel Boone, and the millions of Americans who followed him across the continent, it was always easy to spot the direction to go. Just follow the setting sun and move west. More than any other American, he made possible the settlement of Kentucky, and Missouri as well.

Daniel Boone's Wilderness Road brought Americans by the thousands across the eastern mountains and into the west. It marked the beginning of many another great westward road, including the Santa Fe Trail, the Salt Lake Trail, and the Oregon Trail.

But perhaps he is remembered best for this spirit of adventure. The pioneering spirit of old Daniel Boone and America seem almost as one.

Daniel Boone 1734-1820

1734 Daniel Boone is born on November 2 in Exeter, Berks County, Pennsylvania. First permanent colony in Indiana is settled by eight French families at Vincennes. Eight thousand refugee Protestants from Salzburg, Austria, settle in Georgia.

1735 John Adams, second U.S. president, and Paul Revere, American patriot, are born.

1736 Britain fails to enforce the Molasses Act, as New Englanders continue importing from non-British West Indies islands. Patrick Henry is born.

1737 Thomas Penn angers Delaware Indians by hiring "walkers" to cover land the Indians deeded to William Penn; deed gave Penn all the land a man could walk across in a day; "walkers" walked 66½ miles. Copper money is first coined in Connecticut. William Byrd founds Richmond, Virginia.

1738 British troops are sent to Georgia to settle border dispute with Spain.

1739 Negroes rebel in South Carolina because Spanish missionaries allegedly gave them a false sense of deliverence. England declares war on Spain over their mistreatment of British seamen (War of Jenkins' Ear). English colonists in South Carolina and Georgia declare war on the Spanish in Florida.

1740 War of Austrian Succession, between France, Prussia, Germany, Spain, and England, spills over into colonies as King George's War. Great fire destroys half of Charleston, South Carolina.

1741 Danish explorer Vitus Bering discovers Alaska and dies in a shipwreck. British attack Santiago, Cuba, and seize Spanish treasure ships. Drunkenness is prevalent in colonies, and strict laws are passed against it.

1742 Spanish attack Georgia and are defeated at the Battle of Bloody Marsh on St. Simons Island. Benjamin Franklin invents the Franklin Stove, or Pennsylvania Fireplace.

1743 French explorers reach Rocky Mountains. First white settlement is established in South Dakota. Thomas Jefferson, third U.S. president, is born.

1744 Iroquois League cedes territory in Ohio River valley to England. King Goerge's War begins between British and French colonists when French attack Annapolis Royal, Nova Scotia.

1745 French and Indians raid forts in Maine and burn Saratoga, New York. New England and British troops capture French fort on Cape Breton Island in Canada.

1746 French try unsuccessfully to take Cape Breton and Nova Scotia back from British.

1747 Ohio Company is set up to extend colonial settlements west of Virginia. Britain and France begin competing for control of the Ohio Valley.

1748 Drapers Meadow, first English settlement west of the Allegheny Divide, is founded on the Virginia frontier. King George's War ends with Treaty of Aix-la-Chapelle.

1749 Virginia settlers move into Ohio on land grant from Ohio and Loyal Companies. Negro slavery is extended to Georgia, beginning the South's plantation system.

1750 Boone family leaves Pennsylvania and settles in the Shenandoah Valley in Virginia. Ohio Company sends Christopher Gist, a neighbor of Daniel Boone, to explore the West; he goes down the Ohio River, explores eastern Kentucky, and maps the area. The flatboat, for inland navigation, and the Conestoga covered wagon first appear in Pennsylvania. First American coal mine opens on the James River in Virginia.

1751 Boone family moves to the Yadkin River valley in North Carolina. James Madison, fourth U.S. president, is born.

1752 French begin building forts in Pennsylvania and Ohio to stop British expansion. Benjamin Franklin invents the lightning rod and proves that lightning is electricity. Thomas Bond founds the colonies' first general hospital in Philadelphia.

1753 Governor of Virginia sends George Washington to persuade French to withdraw from Ohio, but the French do not agree.

1754 Representatives of several colonies meet in Albany, New York, to consider a peace treaty with Iroquois Indians; later, French and Indian War begins, with George Washington heading U.S. troops. French defeat Virginia militiamen under Washington at Great Meadows, the first battle of the French and Indian War.

1755 French and Indians defeat Generals Braddock and Washington in Battle of the Wilderness, near Fort Duquesne. Braddock is killed and Washington takes command. British exile 6,000 residents of Acadia on the Bay of Fundy in Canada who will not swear loyalty to Britain. The exiles settle in Louisiana Territory, the name "Acadians" eventually changing to "Cajuns."

1756 Daniel Boone marries Rebecca Bryan. French control Lake Ontario after French General Montcalm captures Fort Oswego. Stagecoach line is established between Philadelphia and New York City.

1757 George Washington acquires his Mount Vernon home. First streetlights (whale-oil lamps designed by Benjamin Franklin) are used in Philadelphia.

1758 George Washington and John Forbes take Fort Duquesne, later renamed Pittsburgh. New British commander James Abercrombie is defeated at Fort Ticonderoga.

1759 Quebec surrenders after French commander Montcalm is killed. Thomas and Richard Penn establish the first recorded life insurance company.

1760 French surrender Detroit to the British. New York requires that all physicians and surgeons pass a test and be licensed to practice medicine.

1761 James Otis opposes British search warrants, saying that they violate the colonists' rights.

1762 France secretly gives Louisiana Territory to Spain to keep British from taking control of it.

1763 Treaty of Paris ends the French and Indian War; Spain gives Florida to Britain; French cede Canadian possessions to Britain. Indians led by Pontiac attack British settlements in Great Lakes region; British King George III issues the Proclamation of 1763 to regulate settlement of the frontier and placate the Indians.

1764 British Parliament passes the Sugar Act to raise money from the colonies. Boston merchants agree to stop purchasing British-made luxury items; all the other colonies follow. First permanent settlement is made at St. Louis, now in Missouri.

1765 British Parliament passes the Stamp Act, the first direct taxation of the colonies, requiring the purchase of tax stamps for all legal documents. Business in the colonies almost comes to a halt when Stamp Act goes into effect. Virginia Assembly challenges Britain's right to tax colonies. Patrick Henry gives his "treason speech," proposing the Virginia Resolutions. Sons of Liberty is organized to force British collection agents to resign. Parliament passes the Quartering Act, requiring colonists to feed and shelter British troops.

1766 British merchants call for repeal of Stamp Act, because of American business failures that resulted. Stamp Act is repealed. New York's refusal to obey Quartering Act leads to clashes between British and colonials. Mason-Dixon Line is drawn between Pennsylvania and Maryland.

1767 Daniel Boone begins exploring west of Appalachian Mountains, traveling along what is now the Kentucky-West Virginia border. Townshend Acts are passed, requiring import duties on tea and other goods.

1768 Cherokee and Iroquois Indians make treaties; Indian lands in Virginia are extended to Ohio River.

1769 Daniel Boone and fellow explorers arrive in Kentucky. British colonial governor abolishes the Virginia Assembly for opposing British taxes. Napoleon Bonaparte is born in Corsica, Italy.

1770 Boston Massacre: British troops kill several colonists in Boston over the issues of the Townshend and Quartering Acts.

1771 British troops suppress an uprising of farmers in North Carolina.

1772 Rhode Island colonists burn the British revenue ship *Gaspee*. Samuel Adams leads the Committees of Correspondence revolt against Britain.

1773 Daniel Boone leads an expedition into Kentucky; Daniel's son James is killed in an Indian attack. Boston Tea Party takes place, in which colonists dressed as Indians dump British tea shipment into Boston harbor.

1774 Massachusetts colonists are punished for Boston Tea Party; Boston port is closed until payment is made for destroyed tea.

1775 Boone, employed by Richard Henderson's Transylvania Company, makes a trail through Cumberland Gap and establishes Boonesborough, Kentucky. Paul Revere makes midnight ride to alert colonists that British troops are on the way to Concord, Massachusetts. American Revolution begins in Lexington and Concord, Massachusetts. George Washington is made commander-in-chief of Continental army. Colonial forces are defeated by British at Bunker Hill.

1776 Congress adopts Declaration of Independence, drafted by Thomas Jefferson. British hang Nathan Hale as a spy, without a trial. Fire destroys much of New York City.

1777 British control Philadelphia; George Washington makes his troops' winter quarters at Valley Forge, Pennsylvania.

1778 Daniel Boone is captured by Indians and adopted by Shawnee chief Black Fish. British capture Savannah, Georgia. James Cook discovers Hawaii.

1779 British surrender to Americans at Vincennes, Indiana.

1780 British capture Charleston, South Carolina. Dutch go to war with Britain.

1781 British General Cornwallis surrenders to Americans in Yorktown, Virginia; American Revolution ends.

1782 British troops evacuate Savannah and Charleston. Holland recognizes U.S. independence. Great seal of the United States is adopted.

1783 American Revolution officially ends in Treaty of Paris, between U.S. and Britain. British troops evacuate New York City.

1784 Thomas Jefferson proposes a plan for governing western territories. North Carolina gives its western territories to the U.S.; eastern Tennessee is called the state of Franklin until 1888, when it becomes part of North Carolina. Deer hunting at night is outlawed in the Carolinas because of many accidental shootings of cattle and horses.

1785 U.S. and Spain dispute over navigation rights on the Mississippi River and over the boundaries of Florida. Thomas Jefferson is appointed minister to France; John Adams becomes minister to Great Britain.

1786 James Madison and Alexander Hamilton form the Annapolis Convention. Massachusetts farmers, led by Daniel Shays, revolt against the state government's high taxes.

1787 Constitutional Convention meets in Philadelphia to draw up the U.S. Constitution; it is signed, and U.S. government is formed. Northwest Ordinance provides for government of Northwest Territory east of the Mississippi River and north of the Ohio River. New York Assembly taxes foreign imports. The dollar becomes the U.S. currency.

1788 U.S. Constitution is ratified by the states and goes into effect. British Parliament moves to abolish slave trade.

1789 First U.S. Congress meets in New York; George Washington is inaugurated president, with John Adams as vice-president, Thomas Jefferson as secretary of state, and Alexander Hamilton as secretary of the treasury. New York City becomes U.S. capital. French Revolution breaks out.

1790 Philadelphia becomes U.S. capital. Alexander Hamilton introduces the U.S. Funding Bill, providing for tariffs and excise taxes to raise revenues for the new United States. Washington, D.C., is founded. Benjamin Franklin dies.

1791 Bill of Rights, the first ten amendments to the Constitution, is ratified. Indians, armed by the British, defeat U.S. forces near Wabash River in Ohio. Vermont becomes the fourteenth state of the Union.

1792 Two U.S. political parties are formed: Republican, by Thomas Jefferson, and Federalist, by Alexander Hamilton and John Adams. Kentucky becomes the fifteenth state. In France, French Republic is proclaimed and Danton seizes power.

1793 Washington and Adams are reelected president and vice-president. Sir Alexander Mackenzie is the first explorer to cross Canada from coast to coast. Fugitive Slave Act requires escaped slaves to return to their owners. Louis XVI and Marie Antoinette are executed in France; Reign of Terror begins.

1794 In "Whiskey Insurrection," Pennsylvania farmers protest liquor tax. U.S. Navy is established.

1795 In Treaty of Greenville, Indians cede land in Northwest Territory to U.S. Florida boundary is set and U.S. gets Mississippi River navigation rights from Spain.

1796 George Washington refuses a third term as president; John Adams defeats Thomas Jefferson in presidential election; Jefferson is elected vice-president. Tennessee becomes the sixteenth state. Congress approves construction of Zane's Trace, a trail from Wheeling, West Virginia, to Limestone, Kentucky.

1797 France obstructs U.S. shipping activities, believing that U.S. is favoring British trade.

1798 Congress orders U.S. navy to take any armed French ships; repeals all treaties with France.

1799 Daniel Boone follows his son Daniel Morgan Boone to Missouri. Hostile Indians obstruct settlement of Mississippi Territory. George Washington dies.

1800 Thomas Jefferson wins presidential election. U.S. capital is moved from Philadelphia to Washington, D.C. Eli Whitney invents muskets with interchangeable parts.

1802 Georgia's western territory is ceded to the U.S. Congress sets up West Point military academy in New York.

1803 In Louisiana Purchase, U.S. buys from France a tract of land extending from Gulf of Mexico to the Northwest. Ohio becomes the seventeenth state.

1804 Alexander Hamilton is killed in a duel with Aaron Burr. Napoleon Bonaparte is crowned emperor of France.

1805 Thomas Jefferson begins second term as president. Michigan Territory, formerly part of Indiana Territory, is established. U.S. and Britain split over West Indies trade.

1806 In Burr Plot, Aaron Burr tries to set up an independent republic in the southwest, but President Thomas Jefferson has him arrested.

1807 Aaron Burr is acquitted in his treason trial. Embargo Act forbids U.S. trade with any foreign countries, in an attempt to force Britain and France to stop interfering with U.S. trade.

1808 U.S. outlaws importing slaves from Africe. U.S. Embargo Act results in merchant protests and smuggling activities.

1809 James Madison becomes the fourth president. Illinois Territory is established.

1810 U.S. annexes West Florida, after revolt against Spanish rule there.

1811 Construction of Cumberland Road begins, from Cumberland, Maryland, to Vandalia, Illinois; completed in 1840, it cost $7 million. William Henry Harrison, later a U.S. president, defeats Indians led by Tecumseh at Tippecanoe, Indiana.

1812 James Madison is reelected president. Louisiana becomes the eighteenth state. U.S declares war on Britain.

1813 British-U.S. battles are fought at Toronto, Fort Niagara, and Lake Erie; British evacuate Detroit.

1814 Andrew Jackson defeats Creek Indians at Battle of Horseshoe Bend, Alabama. U.S. defeats British in Lake Champlain naval battle. British forces burn Washington, D.C.

1815 U.S. defeats Britain in Battle of New Orleans; Treaty of Ghent ends war.

1816 James Monroe and Daniel Tompkins are elected president and vice-president, respectively. Indiana becomes the nineteenth state.

1817 James Monroe becomes fifth U.S. president. Mississippi becomes the twentieth state. Construction of Erie Canal, between Buffalo and Albany, New York, begins.

1818 Canadian-U.S. border is set at the 49th parallel. Illinois becomes the twenty-first state. The *Savannah* is the first steamship to cross the Atlantic.

1819 U.S. purchases Florida and surrounding areas from Spain. Alabama becomes the twenty-second state.

1820 Daniel Boone dies in St. Charles, Missouri. U.S. Land Law sets land prices at $1.25 an acre minimum. Maine becomes the twenty-third state; in "Missouri Compromise," Maine enters the Union as a free state and Missouri (1821) enters as a slave state.

INDEX- *Page numbers in boldface type indicate illustrations.*

Alamance, Battle of, 56
Allegheny Mountains, 21, 27, 30, 31, 38, 39, 59, 61, 65, 67
Allegheny River, 28
American Revolution, 23, 32, 55, 71, 72, 82, 83, 85, 86, 99, 101, 104, 105
Appalachian Mountains, 49
Attakulaculla, 63-65
Audubon, James, 114
Baker, John, 49
Big Hill, 69
Bingham, G. Caleb, **60**
Black Fish, 86, 88-94, 96, 97, 100, 105
Blue Licks, Battle of, 105, 108
Blue Ridge Mountains, 21
Boiling Spring, Kentucky, 72
Boone, Daniel: family background, 11, 12; youth in Pennsylvania, 9, 10, 12-20; in Shenandoah valley, 21-24; in North Carolina, 24, 25; prewar conditions, 25-29; in North Carolina army, 29-33; marriage to Rebecca, 35, 36; in French and Indian War, 37-41; Regulation movement, 42, 43, 56; friendship with Richard Henderson, 43-45; in Florida, 46-48; search for Kentucky, 49-52; exploring Kentucky, 53, 54; moving to Kentucky, 57-59, 63-67; Lord Dunmore's War, 61, 62; building Wilderness Road, 67-70; building Boonesborough, 71, 72; life at Boonesborough, 81-87, 102-106; captured by Black Fish, 87-91; siege of Boonesborough, 92-100; court-martial, 100, 101; as a living legend, 107-109; move to Missouri, 110-112; death of Rebecca, 112; exploring the West, 113; final years, 114, 115
Boone, Daniel (illustrations): **2, 8, 74, 77;** leading pioneers, **60;** captured by Indians, **76;** trying coffin for size, **78**
Boone, Edward (brother), 102, 103
Boone, George (grandfather), 11, 12, 13

Boone, Israel (son), 36, 103, 105
Boone, James (son), 36, 44-46, 52, 58, 59
Boone, Jemima, **74,** 83-85, 87, 89, 91, 96, 100, 112
Boone, Mary (sister), 36
Boone, Nathan (son), 80, 113, 114
Boone, Rebecca Bryan (wife), **34,** 35, 36, 38, 40, 41, 43, 48, 49, 51, 52, 54-57, 61, 81, 82, 91, 101, 104, 108, 112, 113
Boone, Samuel (brother), 16, 102
Boone, Sarah Morgan (mother), 10, 12, 17-19, 41
Boone, Squire (brother), 52, 54, 70, 81, 86, 91, 95, 96
Boone, Squire (father), 10, 12, 15-17, 19-27, 36, 41, 43, **75**
Boonesborough, 72, **73,** 81-105
Boonesborough, Battle of, 95-100
Boston Tea Party, 62
Braddock, Edward, 29-32
British troops, 23, 26, 29-32, 37-39, 55, 56, 86, 88, 90, 92, 100, 101, 103
Bryan, Joseph, 35
Bryan, Rebecca (*see* Boone, Rebecca Bryan)
Bryan, William, 36
Bryan's Station, 104, 105
buffalo herds, 53, 69, 81
Byron, Lord, 107
Callaway, Betsy and Frances, **74,** 83-85, 89, 100
Callaway, Richard, 83-85, 100, 102, 103
Captain Will (Shawnee), 88
Catawba Indians, 27, 29
cemetery, Frankfort, Kentucky, **79**
Charles II, king of England, 11
Cherokee Indians, 40, 41, 54, 55, 61, 63-68, 70, 92, 94, 103
Church of England, 11
Civil War, 21
Clark, George Rogers, 100, 101, 103, 106
Clinch River, 52, 57, 59, 61, 64, 67
Concord, Massachusetts, 71

Concord, Battle of, 71
Congress, U.S., 113
Continental Congress, 82
Cooper, James Fenimore, 107
County of Kentucky, 82
Culpepper, Virginia, 40
Cumberland Gap, 53, 54, 57, 67, 68, 102, 108
Cumberland Mountains, 68
Cumberland River, 53, 65, 69
Cutbirth, Benjamin, 49
Dakotas, 113
Declaration of Independence, 55, 82, 83, 85
Defiance, Missouri, **80**
Delaware Indians, 13-15
Detroit, 85, 90, 92
Discovery, Settlement and Present State of Kentucke, The, 30-31, 99, 107
Dragging-Canoe, 64-67, 69, 103
Dunmore, Lord, 61-63, 71
Elizabethton, Tennessee, 64
England, 11, 12, 25, 26, 27, 46
English troops (*see* British troops)
Exeter, Pennsylvania, 10, 12, 13, 15-18
Femme Osage Creek, 111, 112
Finley, John, 31, 33, 44, 50-54, 68, 99, 107
Florida, 46-49
Forbes, John, 37-39
Forks of the Ohio, 28, 29, 31, 38, 39
Fort Boonesborough (*see* Boonesborough)
Fort Duquesne, 28, 29, 31, 32, 37-40
Fort Necessity, 38
France, 46, 111
Fredericksburg, Virginia, 40
French and Indian War, 28, 36, 37, 40, 45, 46, 50, 85
French troops, 27-29, 32, 33, 38, 39, 92
George III, king of England, 45
Georgia, 46
Granville, Earl of, 25, 57
Gulf of Mexico, 47
Hamilton, Henry, 85, 90, 92
Harding, Chester, 77, 114

Harper, Robert, 21
Harper's Ferry, 21
Harrod, James, 70
Harrodsburg, Kentucky, 72
Henderson, Richard, 43-45, 52, 56, 62-66, 70, 71, 73, 81-83
Henry, Patrick, 104
Iroquois Indians, 65
Jefferson, Thomas, 82, 104, 111
Judgment Tree, 111
Kansas, 113
"Kentucke," 44
Kentucky, 31, 44-46, 49-59, 62-72, 94, 100-109, 113, 114
Kentucky River, 53, 54, 65, 71, 81, 83, 96, 97, 102, 103
Licking River, 54, 87, 89, 100, 105
Lincoln, Abraham (U.S. president), 17
Lincoln, Abraham (U.S. president's grandfather), 17, 102
Lincoln, Mordecai, 17
Little Chillicothe, 90
Logan Station, Kentucky, 72
log cabin, St. Charles County, Missouri, **80**
Longacre, J.B., 77
Long Island, 67
"long handshake," 94, 100
long rifles, 22, 23
Lord Dunmore's War, 61, 62
Louisiana Purchase, 111, 112
Madison, James, 113
Martin, Joseph, 52, 68
Maryland, 29
Massachusetts, 71
Miller, Henry, 13, 15-17, 20, 22-24
Mingo Indians, 92
Mississippi River, 26, 49, 62, 109-111
Missouri, 80, 109-114
Missouri River, 111, 112, 114
Moccasin Creek, 68
Moccasin Gap, 52
Monongahela River, 28, 31, 32

Morgan, Sarah (*see* Boone, Sarah Morgan)
Mount Vernon, 40
Napoleon, 111
Nashville, Tennessee, 82
Nathan Boone House, Defiance, Missouri, **80**
Neversink Mountain, 18
North Carolina, 23-25, 27, 29, 37, 38, 40, 41, 42, 54, 55-57, 62, 63, 64, 71, 91, 92, 101
Northwest Territories, 100
Oconostota, 64
Ohio River, 26, 28, 54, 89, 106, 110
Ohio valley, 29, 38, 39
Oley Township, 16, 18, 19
Onistositah, the Corn Tassel, 64
Oregon Trail, 114
Otter Creek, 71
"Ouasioto," 51
Penn, William, 11, 12
Pennsylvania, 10-12, 14, 15, 19, 21, 22, 24, 29, 30, 35, 36, 38
Pensacola, Florida, 47
Philadelphia, Pennsylvania, 82, 83
Pitt, William, 39
Pittsburgh, Pennsylvania, 39
"plain living," 11
Potomac River, 21
Powell Mountain, 52, 68
Powell valley, 68
Quakers, 11-13, 19, 23, 50
Reading, Pennsylvania, 10
Redcoats, British, 26, 30, 32, 55
Regulation movement, 42, 55, 56
Regulators, 42, 43, 56
revolutionary war (*see* American Revolution)
Richmond, Kentucky, 69
Richmond, Virginia, 104
rifles, long, 22, 23
Rocky Mountains, 27, 113
Russell, Henry, 58, 59
Russell, William, 56-57, 58, 59

St. Augustine, Florida, 47
St. Charles County, Missouri, 80
St. Louis, Missouri, 110
Salisbury, North Carolina, 25, 42, 43
Salt Lake Trail, 114
Santa Fe Trail, 114
Savanooka, the Raven, 64
Schuylkill River, 10
Schuylkill valley, 19
Seminole Indians, 47
Seven Years' War, 46
Shawnee Indians, 13, 15, 27, 29, 58, 59, 61, 62, 65, 68, 70, 83-99
Shenandoah River, 21, 24
Shenandoah valley, 21-24
Six Nations, 65
Society of Friends (*see* Quakers)
South Carolina, 46
Spain, 46, 109-112
Spotswood, Alexander, 21
Stuart, John, 49, 53, 54
Sycamore Shoals, 64
Tennessee, 56, 57, 64, 82
"Ticklicker" (rifle), 25
Tories, 101
Traders' Trace, 46
Transylvania (Kentucky), 82
Transylvania Company, 63, 67, 71, 102
Treaty of Paris, 46
Troublesome Creek, 68
Trudeau, Don Zenon, 109
Virginia, 17, 21-24, 28, 40, 41, 52, 57, 61-64, 71, 82, 85, 87, 92, 100, 102, 104
Walden's Ridge, 52
wampum, 38
Ward, James, 49
Washington, George, 28-32, 38-40, 45, 82, 103
Washington, D.C., 21
Watauga River, 64
West Virginia, 62
"Wide-Mouth" (Boone's nickname), 51, 83, 88

Wilderness Road, 67-69, 71, 102, 107, 108,
   114
Willanaughwa, the Great Eagle, 64
Wyandot Indians, 92, 104, 105
Yadkin River, 23-29, 35, 36, 39, 41-47, 49,

52, 57, 59, 101
Yadkin valley, 23, 24, 28, 36, 38, 40-42, 44,
   45, 47, 49, 50, 57, 101
"Year of the Bloody Sevens," 86, 87
Yellowstone National Park, 113

ABOUT THE AUTHOR

Jim Hargrove has worked as a writer and editor for more than 10 years. After serving as an editorial director for three Chicago area publishers, he began a career as an independent writer, preparing a series of books for children. He has contributed to works by nearly 20 different publishers. His Childrens Press titles are *Mark Twain: The Story of Samuel Clemens, Richard Nixon: The Thirty-seventh President*, and *Microcomputers at Work*. With his wife and teenage daughter, he lives in a small Illinois town near the Wisconsin border.